Comments on other *Amazing Stories* from readers & reviewers

"Tightly written volumes filled with lots of wit and humour about famous and infamous Canadians."
Eric Shackleton, *The Globe and Mail*

"The heightened sense of drama and intrigue, combined with a good dose of human interest is what sets Amazing Stories *apart."*
Pamela Klaffke, *Calgary Herald*

"This is popular history as it should be... For this price, buy two and give one to a friend."
Terry Cook, a reader from Ottawa, on **Rebel Women**

"Glasner creates the moment of the explosion itself in graphic detail...she builds detail upon gruesome detail to create a convincingly authentic picture."
Peggy McKinnon, *The Sunday Herald,* on **The Halifax Explosion**

"It was wonderful...I found I could not put it down. I was sorry when it was completed."
Dorothy F. from Manitoba on **Marie-Anne Lagimodière**

"Stories are rich in description, and bristle with a clever, stylish realness."
Mark Weber, *Central Alberta Advisor,* on **Ghost Town Stories II**

"A compelling read. Bertin...has selected only the most intriguing tales, which she narrates with a wealth of detail."
Joyce Glasner, *New Brunswick Reader,* on **Strange Events**

"The resulting book is one readers will want to share with all the women in their lives."
Lynn Martel, *Rocky Mountain Outlook,* on **Women Explorers**

AMAZING STORIES®

GREAT RIGHT WINGERS

AMAZING STORIES®

GREAT RIGHT WINGERS

Stars of Hockey's Golden Age

HOCKEY

by Monte Stewart

PUBLISHED BY ALTITUDE PUBLISHING CANADA LTD.
1500 Railway Avenue, Canmore, Alberta T1W 1P6
www.altitudepublishing.com
www.amazingstories.ca
1-800-957-6888

Extreme care has been taken to ensure that all information presented in
this book is accurate and up to date. Neither the author nor the
publisher can be held responsible for any errors.

Publisher	Stephen Hutchings
Associate Publisher	Kara Turner
Series Editor	Jim Barber
Editors	Nancy Mackenzie and Marial Shea
Cover and Layout	Bryan Pezzi

We acknowledge the financial support of the Government
of Canada through the Book Publishing Industry Development
Program (BPIDP) for our publishing activities.

Altitude GreenTree Program
Altitude Publishing will plant twice as many trees as were used
in the manufacturing of this product.

Library and Archives Canada Cataloguing in Publication

Stewart, Monte, 1962-
     Great right wingers / Monte Stewart.

(Amazing stories)
Includes bibliographical references.
ISBN 1-55439-086-9

     1. Hockey players--Biography. 2. National Hockey League--Biography.
3. Hockey--Offense. I. Title. II. Series: Amazing stories (Canmore, Alta.)

GV848.5.A1S74 2006   796.962'092'2   C2005-906889-2

Amazing Stories® is a registered trademark of Altitude Publishing Canada Ltd.

Printed and bound in Canada by Friesens
2 4 6 8 9 7 5 3 1

To Dave Leskiw, Ron Wright, Merv Agar,
Danny Roberts, Colin Sloan,
and all of my other hockey buddies.

Contents

Prologue

March 23, 1952. Madison Square Garden, New York City.

The hometown Rangers were leading the Chicago Blackhawks 6–2 early in the third period. Both teams had missed the playoffs and only pride was at stake in this final game of the National Hockey League (NHL) regular season. If the Rangers' lead held up, New York would also claim a moral victory, and rookie goalie Lorne Anderson could improve his chances of staying on with the club. At 20 years old, the Renfrew, Ontario, native was playing in only his third NHL game after being called up from the minors.

It seemed that, years from now, this non-contest would be long forgotten. The Rangers were dominating in all aspects of the game; the Blackhawks did not appear to have any chance of coming back. In fact, it looked like they didn't care who won or lost. But one Chicago player did care. He always cared, even in meaningless games like this one. His name was Bill Mosienko.

Mosienko was the right winger on Chicago's top line, with Gus Bodnar at centre and George Gee on left wing. The trio lined up for the face-off at centre ice after the Rangers scored their sixth goal. Bodnar won the draw and sent it straight to Mosienko. The Winnipeg native darted down the right flank, blew past defenceman Hy Buller like a gust of prairie wind, and ripped a slow wrist shot behind Anderson at 6:09.

It was a nice effort, but the Blackhawks still had little hope of catching up to New York.

Mosienko, Bodnar, and Gee stayed on the ice. In a virtually identical play, Bodnar won the face-off at centre ice again and quickly passed the puck to Mosienko. He undressed Buller again — and scored a second time, at 6:20. Only 11 seconds had passed since the last goal. All of a sudden, with a score of 6–4, New York was down to a 2-point lead.

Mosienko, Bodnar, and Gee lined up once more at centre ice. Could Bodnar pass to Mosienko right from the face-off one more time?

Alas, no. Bodnar did claim the puck again, but he passed it to Gee. The left winger zoomed up the ice — and then passed it to Mosienko. When he got the puck, Mosienko skated toward the goal, calmly deked Anderson to his left — and scored a third goal! The time was 6:30. Mosienko had just scored three goals in 21 seconds. No NHL player had ever done that before.

When the final buzzer sounded, and the Blackhawks posted a remarkable 7–6 victory, the legend of Bill Mosienko was born.

Meanwhile, goaltender Anderson's NHL career was over. He spent the rest of his hockey-playing days in the minor leagues.

Prologue

A half century later, Mosienko's record for the fastest three goals in one NHL game still stands — and almost certainly will never be broken. Not even the great Wayne Gretzky, Gordie Howe, or Rocket Richard could perform such a feat. It only happened because Bill Mosienko refused to lose ...

Chapter 1
Gordie Howe:
From Prairie Boy to
Mr. Hockey

The Red Wings were playing their arch rivals, the Toronto Maple Leafs — and Gordie Howe was ready to pounce on the puck carrier. The date was March 28, 1950. The place was the Olympia Arena in Detroit.

Long before he reached the National Hockey League as a teenager, the big right winger developed a reputation for his physical style. Soon after he entered the NHL with the Red Wings in 1946 at the age of 18, opponents dreaded going into the corner with him because they knew he would likely be the one to come out with the puck.

He wasn't afraid to bang along the boards in the middle of the ice either.

Now, as Toronto's Ted "Teeder" Kennedy lugged the puck up his left wing near the centre red line, Howe raced at him, hoping to deliver a punishing hit. Referee Georges Gravel, sensing an infraction about to happen, already had his arm up to signal a penalty. But the wily Leafs player abruptly stopped — and Howe crashed headfirst into the boards. To this day, people — including the players and coaches who were there — dispute what actually occurred that night.

"They accused me of butt-ending him," Kennedy told author Roy Macskimming in *Gordie: A Hockey Legend*. "But I was a right-handed shot, so the butt of my stick was away from Howe. If there was any contact between us, it was very slight. He'd been going full tilt. He'd been going to run me into the fence. He was the faster skater, he was gaining on me and I knew he was going to get in a good shot. The only thing I was guilty of was getting out of his way."

Wings' coach Tommy Ivan, usually the most mild mannered of bench bosses, yelled and screamed, accusing Kennedy of a dirty hit.

Detroit goalie Harry Lumley supported Kennedy's version. "Gordie went to hit Kennedy but missed him," said Lumley, who watched the incident from his net. "My opinion is that Kennedy simply avoided the check and Gordie hit the boards." One thing was certain: Howe was seriously hurt.

Howe lay prone on the ice, his face covered in blood, as Detroit trainer Carl Mattson jumped over the boards to tend to him. He was carried off on a stretcher and an ambulance, usually kept on stand-by at games, rushed him to Harper Hospital, where doctors determined he had a fractured nose and cheekbone, a badly lacerated eyeball, and hemorrhaging of the brain.

Dr. Frederic Schreiber rushed to the hospital and recommended immediate emergency surgery to avert brain damage — and save Howe's life. Because no relatives were around, Detroit general manager Jack Adams gave approval for the operation. According to Adams, on the way into the operating room, Howe briefly awoke and apologized to Adams. "I'm sorry I couldn't help you more tonight," said Howe.

Reports would say that Howe's skull was fractured, but what actually happened was that Schreiber drilled a hole in Howe's skull just above his right eye and slowly drained fluid that was putting increasing pressure on his brain. It looked like tragedy would ruin the promising career of the can't-miss kid. His mother was called in for what might be her son's final days.

Gordie was born in Floral, Saskatchewan, on March 31, 1928, and grew up in Saskatoon. He'd decided to enter the world while his mother was chopping wood on their farm in Floral, and his father was off completing an excavation job with his horses in Saskatoon, where the family was scheduled to move in a few days. Without the benefit of a midwife or nurse or another adult, Katherine boiled water, got into bed, delivered Gordie, and then cut the umbilical cord. Gordie was the sixth of nine children born to Katherine and Ab Howe.

During Gordie's early years, Saskatchewan was in the throes of the Great Depression. Like many of their neighbours, Gordie's parents would barter for goods. Gordie got his first pair of skates, which he shared with his younger sister Edna, when a neighbour came to the Howes' house in Saskatoon with a sack of goods for sale. The neighbour wanted to sell the goods because her husband was too sick to work and she needed money to feed her baby. Katherine paid $1.50 from the milk money for the sack. The future Wings star got his next pair of skates when his mother traded a pack of Ab's cigarettes to a man who sold goods door-to-door.

Using magazines as shin pads, Gordie learned the game on bumpy frozen sloughs and ponds, a neighbour's backyard rink, and frozen roads. "We could skate on the roads because we had gravel roads with four ruts in them from the cars," recalls Howe in the book *And Howe!* "With the heavy snow, the roads were always covered, and during the day the top of the snow would melt a little bit then re-freeze as nice sheets of ice. So you just stepped out onto those roads. Hell, I could skate anywhere. We'd play after school every day, and on weekends we'd go from early morning to late night."

In response to the constant changes in ice surface, Gordie developed a knack for stickhandling and hanging on to the puck. He played goalie as a youngster and, because he held his stick with his right hand and would have to clear pucks, he learned how to shoot left. As a result, he became ambidextrous, perfecting a powerful backhand that would haunt goalies because they never knew when to expect it.

Gordie had grown to almost 6' and nearly 200 pounds by the time he was in his early teens. Instead of lifting weights, he built his muscles by hoisting 90-pound bags of cement, boulders, and other large objects while working with Ab on construction projects.

On the ice, according to Macskimming, Gordie was "a big, bluff labourer," like Ab, who had come to Canada in search of work and land from Minnesota. Off the ice, he was "gentle and affectionate" like Katherine, "the soft-spoken daughter of German immigrants." Macskimming describes the young Gordie as awkward and shy, and many descriptions of him in his adult years are similar.

His large size appealed to many scouts. As teenage stars like Wayne Gretzky, Mario Lemieux, and Sidney Crosby would do in the future, Howe gained great notoriety in his youth. Unlike these later greats, however, he was a free agent because there was no draft yet. He could sign with any team that wanted him — and several did.

When Gordie was 15 years old he tried out for the New York Rangers. This was a time when many NHL players were fighting overseas, during World War II, and clubs were keen to find new talent. But his awkwardness and shyness led to loneliness when he went to the Rangers' training camp in Winnipeg. No Saskatchewan players travelled on the train with him, and his roommate, a goalie, took a puck in the mouth and left the club. When the camp ended, Gordie became extremely homesick, quit the team even though he was offered a contract, and returned to Saskatoon.

The next year a Detroit scout came calling with another contract. Perhaps because the bird dog had provided Ab with $100, his father told Gordie to hurry up and make up his mind, so he signed.

Gordie did well at the Wings' camp and was sent to a junior affiliate in Galt, Ontario, now part of Cambridge, but he could not play. According to eligibility rules, only a limited number of players from the west were allowed to play in the Ontario Hockey Association, and the Red Wings could not gain permission to use Howe.

Howe spent the season practising with Galt and then moved to Omaha, Nebraska, in the minor-pro United States Hockey League. After one season in Omaha, the next logical step was for him to join Detroit's top farm team in Indianapolis, but the Wings were in a rebuilding mode and Coach Ivan urged general manager Jack Adams to bring Howe to the NHL.

Howe signed a two-way contract that would pay $5,000 if he stayed with Detroit and $3,000 if he went to the minors. With the war having come to an end and financial times still tight, Howe was determined to get the bigger salary. Thinking he was signed for his toughness rather than his scoring ability, he fought as often as possible and recorded more penalty minutes than points in his first three seasons.

In his fourth regular season, just before the playoffs, he had broken loose of his figurative shackles and scored 35 goals while also tallying 33 assists.

Just when his play was turning as many scoring as hitting opportunities, Howe's unfortunate crash into the boards in the game against the Toronto Maple Leafs left him in Harper Hospital. After surgery, with his mother at his side, it appeared that Howe's career was in jeopardy.

The Red Wings, who were trailing 3–0 when Howe left the game, were fired up by the incident. Detroit wound up losing the contest, but the Wings came back and beat Toronto in the seventh and deciding game of the series. Detroit then downed the New York Rangers, also in seven games, for the Stanley Cup.

While the Wings were winning, Howe was making a miraculous recovery. After the final buzzer sounded in the championship game, a determined Howe, now out of hospital, gingerly stepped on the ice while dressed in street clothes, with a fedora hat covering his shaved head and bandages.

Teammate and close friend Ted Lindsay stole the hat, flung it into the crowd like a Frisbee, affectionately rubbed the stubble on Howe's head, and then raised Gordie's arm the way a boxing referee signals a champion prize fighter.

Despite his courageous comeback, Howe was left with a permanent facial tick that caused him to blink repeatedly. As a result, Howe's teammates gave him the nickname Blinky. His recovery from the serious head injury became a testament to Howe's resilience. In future seasons, Howe would excel in spite of injuries and he missed few games.

Howe played an astonishing 25 years — a quarter of a century — in a Red Wings uniform and became the NHL's all-time leading scorer before arthritis in his left wrist caused him to retire from the NHL at age 43 in 1971. He was selected to 21 NHL all-star squads, earning 12 selections to the first team and 9 to the second. He also captured the Art Ross Trophy as the league's scoring leader six times and garnered the Hart Trophy in six seasons, while Detroit won four Stanley Cup titles. He played an astonishing 2,186 regular-season NHL and WHL games and 235 post-season contests.

Howe attributed much of his success to the fine play of his linemates Ted Lindsay and Sid Abel. In 1948–1949, Howe, Lindsay, and Abel became known as the Production Line. The unit was reminiscent of Toronto's famed Kid Line, which featured Charlie Conacher, Busher Jackson, and Joe Primeau, as well as Montreal's heralded Punch Line of Maurice Richard, Elmer Lach, and Toe Blake.

Lindsay was a tough, ornery left winger who upheld Toronto Maple Leafs' owner Conn Smythe's famous credo: If you couldn't beat 'em in the alley, you couldn't beat 'em on the ice. Unlike many of today's so-called grinders, Lindsay was famous for being able to finish plays; he possessed a deft scoring touch.

Abel, the centre, was one of the NHL's most esteemed elder statesmen. He was seven years older than Howe and

Lindsay, who had broken into the league together. Howe and Lindsay were the line's rough rocks while Abel was the polished gem. He personified grace on and off the ice as he tutored Howe and Lindsay the way Lanny McDonald would mentor Joe Nieuwendyk and Gary Roberts many years later with the Calgary Flames. At centre, Abel was the line's playmaker, and he was as fluid with his skating as he was accurate with his passing plays.

Howe was the line's physical force, battling in the corners and sticking up for his teammates every step of the way, but he was also the line's most skilled player. Neither Abel nor Lindsay could skate, score — or scare — the way he could.

Abel and Lindsay were more established than Howe, but he brought out the best in them in that 1948–1949 campaign. Abel, with 54 points, and Lindsay, with 49, finished third and fourth respectively in NHL scoring. Howe, limited to 40 games and 37 points, did not crack the top 10 in scorers — but he would several times in the future.

The next season, the one after Howe sustained his head injury, Lindsay (79 points), Abel (69), and Howe (68), playing in only his fourth NHL season, finished in the top three in league scoring — just as Lach, Richard, and Blake did in the 1944–1945 campaign. If there had been doubt about Howe's ability, there wasn't anymore — he went on to lead the NHL in scoring for the next four seasons.

On January 17, 1951, Howe secured his place in hockey folklore in a game against the Canadiens at the Montreal

Forum. The contest was designated as a special night to honour legendary Montreal winger Maurice "Rocket" Richard, who was then the NHL's greatest goal scorer. Howe stole the show by scoring his 100th career goal, against Gerry McNeil, as Detroit beat Montreal 2–1.

While Howe excelled as a player, the Red Wings also prospered as a team. During those four straight seasons when Howe finished first in scoring, Detroit finished first in the league standings every year — and won four Stanley Cup titles between 1950 and 1955.

On April 1, 1954, in a semifinal game, Howe set the NHL record for the fastest goal to start a game, beating Toronto's Harry Lumley just nine seconds after the opening face-off as Detroit skated to a 4–3 victory in overtime. Howe's feat held up for 27 years, until December 20, 1981 when Doug Smail of the hometown Winnipeg Jets scored in five seconds after the start of their game against the St. Louis Blues. Two other players — Bryan Trottier, then with the New York Islanders (March 22, 1984, against Boston), and Alexander Mogilny, then with the Buffalo Sabres (December 21, 1991, at Toronto), have since tied Smail's record. Heading into the 2005–2006 season, Howe's mark still stood up — 51 years later — as Detroit's team record for the fastest goal from the start of a game.

Howe was one of the main reasons Maurice Richard, despite his many accomplishments, never won a scoring title. Usually, Richard did not win because Howe topped the scoring chart instead. Howe also erased many of Richard's

Gordie Howe

scoring achievements from the NHL record book. Much to Richard's chagrin, some of Howe's most memorable moments — some after the Montreal captain retired — came in games against Les Habitants.

On October 27, 1963, Howe scored his 544th goal against Montreal goaltender Gump Worsley to tie the Rocket's record for the most goals in NHL history. Worsley was in goal again as Howe notched his 600th career goal on November 27, 1965.

Howe reached many of his milestones during the NHL's Original Six era, when the league consisted of only half a dozen clubs. In 1967–1968, the league expanded to 12 teams, and the increase in players was supposed to lead to an increase in talent — and make the circuit more competitive. Howe continued to thrive, and on December 4, 1968, notched his 700th career goal versus goaltender Les Binkley of the Pittsburgh Penguins.

On April 3, 1971, as Detroit celebrated the 25th anniversary of Olympia Arena, Howe scored the 786th goal of his career against Chicago's butterfly-specializing goaltender, Tony Esposito. It was Howe's final goal as a Red Wing. He retired from the NHL at the end of that season.

Howe was never the NHL's highest paid player. While general manager Adams rewarded Howe with a $1,000 raise each season, his teammate Ted Lindsay, as tough at the bargaining table as he was on the ice, earned much more, as did several other players.

Upon his retirement, the Wings rewarded Howe with a cushy vice-president's posting, but as many veterans discover in their first seasons away from the action, he did not like being off-ice.

Howe retired at a time when hockey was going through a revolution. For the first time in hockey history, Canada's NHL stars played an eight-game summit series in 1972 against the Soviet Union. The upstart World Hockey Association (WHA), led by a marketing specialist named Dennis Murphy, had started up and raided the NHL's top players, such as Chicago left winger Bobby Hull and Boston goalie Gerry Cheevers. The WHA also shocked many observers by welcoming European stars like Anders Hedberg and Ulf Nilsson, and by revising the rules, eliminating the centre red line to allow for a more free-flowing offensive game.

Three years after his last game with the Wings, Howe came out of retirement. He added to the WHA's uniqueness as he underwent surgery to repair his wonky wrist and joined the Houston Aeros — and brought his teenage sons Mark and Marty with him. Never before had a pro player toiled with one son, let alone two.

Howe received $1 million from the four-year deal negotiated by wife Colleen while Mark and Marty each earned about $600,000. By signing, Howe defied a request from NHL president Clarence Campbell to prevent Mark and Marty from signing with the rival WHA.

Houston coach Bill Dineen happened to be a former Detroit teammate, but he was also a stickler for conditioning. With Howe struggling to get back in shape, the coach decided to hold two practices per day. Howe felt like his return to pro hockey was a big mistake. The two practices a day were onerous. However, Coach Dineen's ploy worked; after a few days, Howe got his legs back.

Coach Dineen added to the buzz of the Howes' signing by putting them on a line together. In the NHL, Gordie was known for sticking up for his teammates along the side and corner boards, but he frowned even more when infractions were committed against his sons, who called him Gordie on the ice.

When Edmonton Oilers goon Roger Cote punched Mark and landed on top of him during a line brawl, Gordie politely asked him to let Mark get up.

Cote responded with a profanity. Gordie promptly stuck his fingers in Cote's nostrils and pulled him up.

"Okay, I'm up. I'm up," said Cote, pleading for mercy.

"The guy's nose must have stretched half a foot," recalled Marty.

Gordie did more than just fight for Mark and Marty. He also set them up for many goals — and scored several himself. Now that he had resumed playing hockey, Howe resumed setting records — and they came quickly: November 3, 1973, he netted his first WHA goal and 787th all-time marker; January 17, 1974, he counted his 800th career goal against Peter Donnelly of the Vancouver Blazers; March 17, 1975, he recorded the 2,000th point of his pro hockey career — 15 years after he had recorded his 1,000th career point, on November 27, 1960, with Detroit.

In 1973–1974, the Howes were arguably the WHA's best line as the Aeros won the inaugural Avco Cup as league champions.

Gordie also made up for missing the 1972 Summit Series by playing for a WHA-based Canadian team in September of 1974.

During his first WHA season, while he was driving into a hotel parking lot, Howe saw a man snatch a woman's purse. He chased the culprit for several blocks before the man dumped the bag. Gordie wanted to keep going after him, but his wife, Colleen, forbade him. When he returned the purse to the woman, her friend asked how they could repay him for his heroism. "Well, I'm a player with the Houston Aeros," said Gordie. "How about attending some of our games?" The woman and her friend promised to become regular fans. Other spectators were not as loyal, even though the Aeros won their second straight Avco Cup. The fickle fans preferred to watch pro and college football, baseball, and basketball instead, and the Houston franchise struggled financially. Some Aeros were not paid, but the Howes still received their cheques.

In 1976–1977, Gordie, Mark, and Marty moved to the New England Whalers, based in Hartford, Connecticut, and coached by Harry Neale, now a Hockey Night in Canada analyst. Gordie counted 96 points, but the league as a whole was approaching its deathbed. As the Howes began their second season with the Whalers, franchises moved, folded, and struggled to pay players, especially their stars. Rumours that the WHA would merge with the NHL became stronger every day.

On, March 2, 1977, Howe scored his 900th major league goal, and just nine months later, on December 7, 1977, he produced his 1,000th professional goal against John Garrett of the Birmingham Bulls, who would go on to become a hockey commentator on television and radio — and tell many stories about Howe.

One historic night, January 2, 1979, when they were in the WHA, Howe and Wayne Gretzky played on a line together, along with Mark Howe. Gordie Howe had been Gretzky's idol growing up and the centre wore 99 because he did not want to insult Howe and the other stars who wore number nine. It was the WHA all-stars against the famed Russian team, Moscow Dynamo, which was touring North America. Gordie was 50; Gretzky was 17. The game, played in Edmonton, was only 35 seconds old when Gretzky put in an easy rebound after Gordie and Mark had buzzed the net. Gordie recorded two assists as the WHA all-stars doubled Dynamo 4–2. The Howes and Gretzky played together in two more games against Moscow Dynamo. The WHA squad posted 4–2 and 4–3 victories, sweeping the three-game series.

Howe was limited to 58 games because of injuries that season, and tallied just 43 points, one less than the 44 he counted in his sophomore season with Detroit. At the end of the season, the now rampant rumours became reality. The WHA ceased operations and the NHL agreed to accept some teams from the rival organization — including the Hartford Whalers.

Eight years after he was supposedly too old to play for Detroit, Howe returned to the league where he had starred for so many years. At the age of 51, he was arguably more popular than Gretzky, who was playing his first NHL season with the Edmonton Oilers. Gretzky's first season in the league was Howe's last, so they did not get on the ice together with the NHL as often as they had with the WHA.

On another memorable night, February 5, 1980, at Howe's shrine — the Olympia in Detroit — they squared off against each other in the annual all-star game.

Howe only played because Prince of Wales Conference coach Al Arbour added him to the roster to comply with rules that required all teams to be represented in the game. Gretzky was voted on to the Clarence Campbell squad because of his stellar play in his rookie campaign.

Although he was no longer the player he used to be, the night clearly belonged to Howe. When players were introduced, he received the largest ovation, and fans cheered wildly as he assisted on Real Cloutier's goal at 16:06 of the third period as their Wales Conference team skated to a 6–3 victory over Gretzky's Campbell squad.

Whenever the Whalers visited Canadian rinks, they were sold out and temporary fences had to be put up as hordes of fans clamoured for Howe's autograph. On April 11, 1980, Howe, at 52 and 10 months, became the oldest player to suit up for an NHL game. Again, his resilience paid off: he played in all 80 regular-season games, producing 41 points and recording a plus-nine mark, meaning he was on the ice for nine more goals scored than goals against.

Howe scored 15 goals in his final NHL season, but he still helped Hartford win one more game than the Red

Wings, who were going through one of the worst periods in their illustrious history. Fittingly, on April 6, 1980, he scored the final goal of his pro career against the Red Wings. Howe helped Hartford make the playoffs and counted two points in three games — his last in the NHL.

If he wasn't already, Howe has become hockey's greatest ambassador during his retirement, confirming his nickname of Mr. Hockey. He has appeared at countless events, including hockey, ringette, and golf tournaments, plus many awards banquets, raising millions of dollars for various charities through the Howe Foundation, which he and Colleen launched in 1993.

Wherever he goes, hundreds of children, many of whom never saw him play, line up to get his autograph or shake his hand — along with their parents, who cheered for him when they were youngsters. "They always tell you when you meet your heroes and idols, you walk away saying, 'Well, they're not that nice, or just okay,'" said Gretzky, who was 12 when he met Howe. "But Gordie, he was bigger and better than I ever imagined."

Howe has also endorsed many products, including a line of athletic clothing that bears his name, earning much more than he ever did in his prime as a player.

In 1995, he told the story of his playing days in *And … Howe!* with co-author Tom Delisle. Howe published the book himself through an aptly named company, Power Play Publications, which he and Colleen created with help from his Calgary-based agent, Wayne Logan, who also represents authors. The book became a bestseller, with thousands of copies sold. Howe also told the story of his retired life in the book *After the Applause.*

As the years passed, Gretzky broke Howe's all-time scoring record and most of his other milestones, but never surpassed his mark of 975 goals scored in the NHL and WHA, and would never come close to his games played total.

Barring unexpected comebacks long after their playing days have ended, Gretzky and virtually all other players will never break one record that Howe set in 1997. At the age of 69, he signed a one-game contract with the Detroit Vipers of the now-defunct International Hockey League.

Howe credits much of his success to his wife Colleen, who served as his agent for many years and became the first woman inducted into the U.S. Hockey Hall of Fame in Minnesota. At the age of 69, Mrs. Hockey was diagnosed with Pick's disease, a progressive form of dementia, named after German neurologist Arnold Pick, which alters a person's personality and character. The incurable malady strikes people as young as 20 and as old as 80 — but mostly people in their 50s and 60s, like Colleen Howe.

Howe has curtailed some of his activities in recent years, in order to care for Colleen, but he continues to travel to appearances throughout North America as often as possible. "I know Colleen would want me to continue meeting the fans and promoting the greatest game," said Howe. In other words, he is determined to overcome adversity, just as he did one night long ago, in March of 1950.

By the time he retired, in the NHL and WHA combined, Howe recorded 975 regular-season goals, 1,423 assists, and 2,358 points in 2,186 regular-season games and another 231 points in 235 playoff games. He finished at or near the top of league scoring in the NHL or WHA — in each of the four decades he played, from the 1940s through the 1970s. While many pundits don't like to compare players from different eras, they can assess Howe this way because he played in so many different eras.

Howe was on the ice from the end of World War I to the first expansion of the NHL to the merger with the WHA to the rise of the phenom named Gretzky. He was there from the time most players used straight sticks to the time when most used curves … from the days when goalies did not wear masks and players, like himself, did not wear helmets to the days when helmets became mandatory and goalies would not dare play without face shields. He was also there from the time when hockey was a game played by Canadian players to the time when the first Europeans began playing pro in North America. He was there from the days of rhythm and blues to the days of rock and roll to the days of punk rock. Howe outlasted NHL presidents and American presidents and Canadian prime ministers and premiers.

There will, almost certainly, never be another player like Gordie Howe.

Chapter 2
Howie Meeker: The Kid from Kitchener

ven if you have never heard of Howie Meeker, chances are someone in your family knows of him.

Long before Don Cherry became a household name, Meeker graced Hockey Night in Canada and The Sports Network (TSN) telecasts with his enthusiasm, encyclopedic knowledge of the game, and tell-it-like-it-is style. Kids from coast to coast would repeat his unique expressions — like "golly-gee-willikers," "five-hole," and "put it upstairs" (shoot high over the sprawling goalie) — as they impersonated him while playing street hockey. During his 30-year broadcasting career, he became famous for his short greyish hair, wire-framed glasses, squeaky voice, and a smile as bright as a lighthouse. He was more recognizable — and probably more famous — than most of Canada's prime ministers.

Meeker the commentator made the now common telestrator famous as he drew diagrams on replays — right on your TV screen — and hollered at invisible technicians in the mobile studio truck to "stop it right there" and "back it up." His on-air skills earned him a place in the Hockey Hall of Fame, but the truth is, Howie Meeker was more than just a broadcaster. He was also coach, general manager, administrator, soldier, and Member of Parliament (MP). Meeker also operated his own hockey school and hosted a TV show.

But first, he was a hockey player.

Meeker was born in Kitchener, Ontario, in 1923. He grew up in the nearby town of New Hamburg and developed a passion for the game after learning to skate at the age of three. Meeker worked as a stick boy for a senior team in Kitchener-Waterloo and developed his skills on his family's backyard rink, a local lake, schoolyard rinks, and other arenas across southern Ontario. All along, he dreamed of playing for his beloved Toronto Maple Leafs of the National Hockey League.

Although he was small for his age, the right winger excelled against kids who were older and bigger.

When Meeker was a teenager, as author Charlie Hodge reports in his excellent biography *Golly Gee – It's Me!: The Howie Meeker Story*, he starred for the New Hamburg Hahns and junior clubs in Kitchener, Brantford, and Stratford. In

1941–1942, he compiled 45 points in only 13 regular-season games with Stratford.

In those days, junior leagues did not draft bantam and midget age players as they do now. Rather, players became the property of junior teams closest to their homes.

One year, Waterloo and Stratford teams both wanted Meeker to play for them. Waterloo claimed he was their property because New Hamburg was closer to Waterloo than Stratford. The Ontario Hockey Association (OHA) ordered a measurement "portal to portal" and Waterloo was, indeed, found to be closer.

Meeker, however, preferred to play for Stratford. Waterloo manager Beland Honderich, who would later become publisher of the *Toronto Star*, asked Meeker to skate with Waterloo for a couple of weeks and then see if he liked the club. In a rare move, after Meeker finished his two-week trial, Honderich granted his request for release and Meeker returned to Stratford, where his club won an OHA Junior "B" championship in 1941–1942.

"We were 16- and 17-year-old kids with our pictures in the newspapers and programs, being interviewed on radio along with two big parades, including bands, fire trucks, and thousands of fans at the rallies," Meeker told author Hodge. "Jeez, it wouldn't be hard to think you were a 'somebody.'"

The next day, he returned to being a nobody as he went back to work for the Canadian National Railway (CNR). "I can still hear that damn [start-work] bell going ding, ding,

ding," recalls Meeker. "Then I'd climb into my dirty, greasy overalls and head off to find my partner and spend the next eight hours in grease up to my armpits, dismantling a 6400 locomotive in for a refit — all for 18 cents an hour."

Somewhat foolishly, Meeker suggests, he had convinced his mother to allow him to quit school when he was only 13 years old so that he could help his family make ends meet during the Great Depression of the 1930s.

Meeker knew he would not spend his life working on the railroad, but after an unfortunate turn of events in September of 1942, he was happy just to be alive. He and his buddies were driving to Niagara Falls on the Labour Day weekend when he suddenly felt a terrible pain in his stomach.

They stopped for help at a clinic in Hamilton — just in time. After a brief examination, a doctor shipped Meeker to hospital and he underwent emergency surgery.

"I guess I damn near died that night, my appendix had ruptured, spilling infection all through my body," says Meeker.

Three weeks later, he returned to the ice and continued to gain the notice of scouts. The Leafs owned his NHL rights and one Sunday morning they summoned him to Toronto for a practice. In the dressing room, as he took off his street clothes and put on his hockey gear, Meeker, only 18 years old at the time, thought to himself, "Ah, jeez, this can't be true, I gotta be dreaming."

After skating alongside such legends as Bucko

McDonald, Dave "Sweeney" Schreiner, Bob Davidson, Babe Pratt, Lorne Carr, and scoring on the great goalie Turk Broda, Howie knew he could play at the NHL level. He was certain he would one day have a regular stall in the Leafs' historic dressing room at Maple Leaf Gardens.

But a few months later, with World War II raging in Europe, Meeker's life took a different turn. Like thousands of other young Canadian men, he felt he had a duty to serve his country, so at the age of 19, he joined the Canadian army.

Hiding his skates in his baggage, he shipped overseas to the English countryside.

As a result of his experience in the CNR shops, he landed in the Canadian Engineers' Corps. These soldiers had received little training in warfare and were expected to stay far away from the front as they learned how to repair different makes of trains. However, Meeker's senior officers decided that the company should go through military maneuvers.

During an exercise over two large farms that involved taking a hill from the enemy, another Canadian soldier mistakenly tossed a live grenade over a rock fence at Meeker — and it exploded. Four large pieces of metal lodged in his right leg and a combined total of 40 smaller pieces embedded in both lower limbs. After doctors cut the metal out of his legs, gangrene set in, a disease that, if not treated properly, could result in amputation.

The dejected Meeker wrote a letter to Hap Day and suggested the Leafs' coach take his name off Toronto's protected list — because he didn't think he'd be playing hockey anymore, or doing much of anything for a while.

Meeker spent eight weeks in the hospital wondering what would become of his life. With help from skilled surgeons, and good fortune, Meeker avoided permanent injury. His wounds healed and he began training as a physical education instructor at a base at Shorncliffe, Kent, near Folkestone on the south coast of England.

On the last day of his three-week course, Meeker's final assignment was to run with full battle kit and 10 pounds of sand in his knapsack. To his surprise, his legs didn't cause any problems. He discovered he could run all day on them. The problem was his upper body — he had to carry his knapsack, steel helmet, and rifle, which stuck into him wherever he tried to place it. As he ran up the hill, tears welled up in his eyes as he hoisted his gear. When he finished, he felt a great sense of pride — which he would not soon forget.

The war had a profound effect on Meeker. He now felt he was a much better person and far more prepared for anything in life. Army life had also made him more disciplined. As the war came to an end, he felt like he could do anything he wanted. All it would take was hard work and courage.

Meeker applied that attitude when he arrived home in New Hamburg in late December of 1945. After just a dozen regular-season and playoff games with a Stratford senior team, he received a contract offer from the Maple Leafs and signed for $4,500 a year plus a $2,000 bonus on April 13, 1946.

Meanwhile, he married his high school sweetheart, Grace, to whom he had proposed before going overseas.

In the fall of 1946, Meeker advanced from Toronto's rookie camp and, playing alongside the heroes of his youth, survived the main training camp. He was placed on a line with left winger Vic Lynn, a fellow rookie, and veteran centre Ted "Teeder" Kennedy.

The line even earned the praise of Conn Smythe, the Leafs' fiery president, who dished out compliments as often as a tax auditor distributes refunds. "Here you have Lynn, the hewer of wood and carrier of water; Kennedy the brains; Meeker the killer to finish off," Smythe told the *Globe and Mail* after they had been playing together for a few years.

As Meeker's point production declined, he was noted more for his physical play, but he still produced timely goals. Sometimes his goals and fights occurred minutes apart.

In a December 27, 1947, tight-checking game against the Rangers at Madison Square Garden in New York, Meeker scored early in the second period to give the Leafs a 1–1 tie. Later in the period, Meeker tangled with Tony Leswick, a player who was about the same size.

When Leswick high-sticked him, Meeker responded by shoving him — in the face — and then picked him up and body slammed him to the ice just like Whipper Billy Watson, a popular wrestler of the same era.

Leswick banged his head on the ice and skated woozily to the dressing room where he spent the rest of the period.

He came back in the third period with a large bandage on his noggin.

Meeker also showed Detroit winger Gordie Howe why he should concentrate on scoring instead of fighting. In the second game of the Stanley Cup finals on April 11, 1948, Howe decided that he'd had enough of Meeker's shenanigans and dropped the gloves with his fellow right winger.

Howe pulled Meeker's sweater over his shoulders and unloaded a series of jabs with both fists. Meeker lost the battle, but he helped the Leafs win the war. With Howe sitting in the penalty box for five minutes, along with Meeker, Toronto scored three goals and skated to a decisive 4–2 victory.

The Red Wings, who had lost a close 5–3 decision in the first game, never recovered from the setback and the Leafs swept the series 4–0 to claim their second of three straight Stanley Cups. Howe learned from the incident with Meeker. He soon stopped fighting as often and became the NHL's greatest scorer until Wayne Gretzky came along decades later.

Meeker had many memorable nights that rookie season, but a game against Chicago on January 8, 1947, stood out from most as he scored five goals in a 10–4 win over the Blackhawks.

He almost didn't get credit for the first two as slapshots from defenceman Wally Stanowski went in off his stick and bum. Coach Day ensured that the official scorekeeper gave the goals to Meeker.

At the time of this writing, only one other rookie in the

NHL's modern era — Don Murdoch of the New York Rangers — has matched Meeker's rookie accomplishment of five goals in one game.

By the end of the season, Meeker set a rookie record for goals, with 27, and added 18 assists to finish 15th in league scoring. Those numbers, along with 76 penalty minutes (10th highest in the league), enabled him to beat out heralded newcomer Gordie Howe of the Detroit Red Wings for rookie of the year honours.

Meeker was the Theoren Fleury of his era. His approach to the game — and to life — was simple. He wanted to have fun. Although he was only 5'8", Meeker had unusually large feet and wore size 11 skates. You would think his big fins would slow him down as he fluttered along the ice, but they didn't. He strived to maintain excellent balance and was arguably the fastest Leafs player.

He felt he was great without the puck because he knew what to do defensively and concentrated on that side of the game. By his own admission, his feet were faster than his brain, so any goal he got was a bonus.

Despite Meeker's shortcomings and lack of experience in his first season, Coach Hap Day used him in the most difficult situations, against the NHL's greatest players. As the clock ticked down in the sixth and deciding game of the 1947 Stanley Cup finals, Day sent Meeker out against Montreal's fabled Punch Line of Maurice "Rocket" Richard, (the league's second-leading scorer that season), Elmer Lach, and Toe

Blake. Meeker could not look to any veteran Leafs for guidance because all the other Toronto players — Ted Kennedy and Vic Lynn at forward and Nick Metz and Jim Thompson on defence — were also rookies.

The Leafs were leading the series 3–2 and struggling to hold on to a precarious 2–1 advantage in the game. Meeker and his mates held the Habs in check and Toronto claimed the Stanley Cup.

Meeker may have been smaller than Howe, but he had a style of play all his own. He thrived on speed, hustle, determination, and physical play. Still, Meeker downplayed his supremacy over future superstar Howe in this first pro season.

"I was 22 years old and Gordie was just 17; he was not even in the running at that point," says Meeker, who often fought with Howe. "He was really just a kid and you knew he was going to be a great player some day. It's not fair to Gordie to compare us like that. He was a big, tough, talented boy who needed a few years to bloom. I was a man back from a war. Five years later, I was getting 7 goals and he was getting 37."

Meeker continued his scrappy play in his first post-season as the Leafs defeated the fabled Montreal Canadiens for the first of three consecutive Stanley Cup championships. Although he was still part of the team, he did not share in the third Cup as he missed most of the regular season with a shoulder injury sustained in practice and a broken foot that kept him out of the playoffs.

Meeker played in the NHL all-star game in each of his first three seasons. But his role was changing as his offensive output began to decline (even though he was 17th in NHL scoring in 1949–1950).

After waging a contract dispute with Toronto general manager Conn Smythe, he began recording plus-minus rates and other important statistics in a notebook and started studying the nuances of the game. "You can be a student of mistakes as long as you do something about them," he once told Al Nickleson of the *Globe and Mail.*

In a February 25, 1950 game against the New York Rangers, Meeker waged another memorable battle as he fought a tough ex-Royal Canadian Mounted Police (RCMP) officer named Gus Kyle. The two fell to the ice and then, according to Meeker, Kyle tried to gouge the little right winger's eyes out. Kyle was much bigger and much heavier, and Meeker's arms were pinned. He knew he had to do something, so he bit one of Kyle's thumbs.

The big Ranger howled in pain and ceased and desisted like an arrested criminal.

"That's the first time anyone bit me," Kyle complained in the penalty box.

Meeker later told the *Globe and Mail* that Kyle's thumb wasn't that tough.

Meeker often played in pain because of a lingering back problem and numerous injuries, some of which even occurred in practice. On Boxing Day of 1948, he suffered a broken collarbone during a Leafs workout, when he stepped on Bill Ezinicki's stick, and missed several weeks of action. You could call that a friendly mishap, but Meeker's aggravating ways sidelined him again, in February of 1949, only three games after he had returned to action. The pesky winger got into a skirmish with Bill Gadsby in a game against the Blackhawks at Chicago Stadium. An irate Gadsby swung his stick at Meeker's head, but Meeker ducked and the stick came crashing down on his foot instead. He suffered a broken foot, which kept him out of the 1948–1949 playoffs, while the Leafs won their third consecutive Stanley Cup. In the 1950–1951 regular season, he blew out a knee, but still managed to stay in shape during the several weeks he was sidelined.

The Leafs were hit by injuries while he was out. At one time, he was one of five players sidelined because of ailments. Some players were close to returning around the same time, but according to the *Globe and Mail*, Meeker looked to be in the best shape of the bunch.

His fitness paid off in the playoffs as, showing no ill effects from his knee injury, which had limited him to only 49 games in the regular season, Meeker won a race that resulted in him setting up one of the most memorable goals in Leafs history.

While Montreal's Tom Johnson was ramming him hard into the boards behind the net, Meeker passed the puck out front and, while Meeker could not see what was happening,

Bill Barilko scored to give the Leafs the Stanley Cup — their fourth in five years.

After Barilko scored the historic goal, he kissed his mother near centre ice, and later sipped champagne with his teammates in the dressing room. Although Barilko was the hero of the moment, his memorable goal only occurred because of Meeker's hustle to the puck. (This was to be Barilko's last goal. Sadly, he died that summer in a plane crash after setting out for a fishing trip in northern Ontario.)

Since NHLers received modest salaries back then, Meeker had spent previous summers working on a railroad and at other jobs. Shortly after returning to New Hamburg, he received an offer he hadn't expected.

Eal Katzenmeier, an insurance agent who organized the town's horseracing derby and also dabbled in politics, urged Meeker to run for parliament as a Conservative. Meeker had no political experience, no knowledge, and no interest, but Katzenmeier was persistent. So was Meeker's father, Charlie, who was a staunch Tory. When Meeker and his wife Grace went on a fishing trip, leaving their baby daughter Jane at home with her grandparents, George Drew, leader of the Conservatives (then the official opposition), rolled up in the woods in a big white Cadillac and asked Meeker to run.

"If I was to run and I lost, who would pay my campaign costs?" asked Meeker. "The nomination fee is $250 and if I don't get a certain percentage of the vote I'll lose money. Besides, I make $7,000 a year playing hockey and you only get

$3,000 a session and $2,000 tax-free in parliament. I've got no education, no rich parents, no big business, and no interest. The only thing I know is hockey and I can't take a pay cut."

Drew convinced Meeker to go with him to a phone and dialed up Leafs general manager Conn Smythe, a hero of World War I who was also a loyal Conservative. To Meeker's surprise, the notoriously cheap Smythe promised that, if he ran, he would pay his hockey salary — even if he couldn't play. So Meeker ran — gaining from his popularity as a hockey player — defeating the closest rival, Norm Moffatt of the Liberals, who was a former mayor of Galt, by 2,553 votes. At 27 years of age, Meeker became Canada's youngest MP.

Meeker, however, had no plans to stop playing for the Leafs. He haggled with Smythe for a new contract that paid $10,000 per year, thinking he would play part time, depending on when he could get away from his political duties. Instead of going home to New Hamburg on weekends, he would go to wherever the Leafs were playing.

On the ice, Meeker became known as Your Honour and the Senator (even though neither moniker was an accurate description for an MP), and still managed to play a lot of games, when he wasn't injured.

Meeker left politics in 1953 after one term and, as injuries took their toll and his goals declined even more, he began thinking about retiring as a hockey player. A back injury forced him out of the NHL in 1953 — at the age of 29 — and he embarked on a coaching career with a Stratford senior team while also opening a jukebox business that was tied to his coaching contract.

During a brief three-game comeback with the Leafs, Hap Day, now a Leafs executive, asked Meeker if he would be interested in a coaching position in Toronto's organization some day. At the end of the season, Day invited Meeker to become the bench boss of their farm club in Pittsburgh. Although he had been offered a half ownership interest in the Stratford club, and stood to make less money when he factored in his 50 percent share in the jukebox business, Meeker agreed to coach Pittsburgh in the rat-infested Duquesne Gardens.

Meeker guided the Hornets to the Calder Cup and, after one more season, was offered the Leafs job for the 1956–1957 campaign. Toronto missed the playoffs under Meeker but, after Hap Day quit following a dispute with the cantankerous Smythe, Meeker the coach was promoted to general manager (GM).

Meeker only lasted as GM until November of 1958, as Smythe's son Stafford — whom Meeker punched in the nose after an argument — was in the process of taking over the club. Rather than join another NHL team, Meeker made an unusual move. He accepted a five-year contract to become head coach of all teams in the United Church Athletic Association, who were known as the Guards, in St. John's, Newfoundland. He had tested out the climate on the Rock for a few months with a junior all-star team — after Newfoundland Premier

Joey Smallwood urged him to consider a vague position that had been offered. "Newfoundland was an experience like no other, and I'm glad we didn't pass it up, tempted as I was on those first couple of flights to Newfoundland to just head home," says Meeker.

In addition to coaching, he opened a sporting goods store and launched his career as a sportscaster as he hosted a show on CJON Radio. Meeker became a member of Prime Minister John Diefenbaker's National Sports Advisory Council — and briefly played for a St. John's team that competed for the provincial championship.

Before leaving Newfoundland, Meeker would also start up a school-based minor hockey association, launch a midget-juvenile league run by RCMP officers, and open an agency that sold bowling equipment, luggage, Lego, toys, guns, and other products.

As millions of Canadians were bringing televisions into their homes in the early 1960s, Meeker hosted a bowling TV show and began working on Hockey Night in Canada. He also started his hockey school and a related show on CBC TV.

Soon, he started receiving invitations to operate clinics in cities and towns across the country. One came from Parksville, British Columbia, a small town near Nanaimo on Vancouver Island.

Meeker fell in love with the picturesque island scenery. Tired of Newfoundland's harsh weather, he and Grace moved their family to Parksville after purchasing property overlooking the Pacific Ocean. Meeker still lives there with his second wife, Leah, whom he married in 1999 after Grace, a long-time smoker, died of a heart attack in January of 1998.

In Parksville, Meeker has played in oldtimers' games, organized hockey tournaments, and lent his name to many charitable causes, including an annual golf tournament for BC Guide Dogs. As a result of his efforts, town and regional district officials named the Howie Meeker Arena in his honour. At first, Meeker was against the idea of having a rink in his name, because he felt that he had not done enough for hockey in the area, but he later relented.

In the summer of 2005, he arranged for the Stanley Cup to visit Parksville as part of its annual summer tour, helping hockey-starved fans get a fix on their NHL addiction while the players' lockout was still in effect. More than 1,000 fans turned out to meet Meeker, now in his 80s, and get their picture taken with the Cup.

The event was chronicled on the Hockey Hall of Fame's Web site. The gregarious Meeker indicated he won't be stopping such activities anytime soon. "Let me tell ya sumthin' — it's been one hell of a life and I ain't through yet," said Meeker.

Meeker has captivated hockey fans from coast to coast for more than 60 years. He was a household name when Gordie Howe was a rookie and Rocket Richard was in his heyday, when Bobby Clarke was leading Philadelphia's Broadstreet Bullies, when Wayne Gretzky and Mario Lemieux emerged as superstars, and when a kid named Sidney Crosby broke into the NHL. Meeker won the Calder Trophy and four Stanley Cups in only eight seasons, helping to set standards that would haunt the modern-day Leafs. He did things his way, from the time his team won the Memorial Cup, to the time he scored five goals as a rookie, assisted on Bill Barilko's Stanley Cup-winning goal, was a quick-skating MP, coached and managed the Maple Leafs, built Newfoundland's minor hockey system — and to the many times he showed up on TV sets in people's living rooms.

Unlike many of his predecessors and successors who have appeared on camera, Meeker refused to apologize for the shortcomings of a league often criticized for its lack of creativity. Whether he was playing, coaching, managing, commenting, or teaching, he won the hearts and souls of the young and old alike. No matter how they know about him, Canadians won't soon forget the name Howie Meeker.

Chapter 3
Andy Bathgate: Humble Hall of Famer

Many players who reach the National Hockey League can thank their fathers for getting them there. Dads have a way of pushing their boys to excel, and in many cases, sons have followed their fathers into the league. Some examples are Mark and Gordie Howe and Brett and Bobby Hull.

Andy Bathgate was not so fortunate. He was only 13 when his father died of throat cancer in the mid-1940s. Although Andy could not rely on his father to show him the way to the Stanley Cup finals, he still got there — and changed the course of history.

Three years after his father died, and with the rest of the Bathgates in difficult financial straits, Andy and his mother decided to leave Winnipeg. Andy, who had played most of his minor hockey outdoors during frigid Manitoba winters, and his mother, originally from Toronto, went to Guelph, Ontario.

In doing so, Andy passed up an offer to play on a Winnipeg junior team for $100 per season. They went to Guelph because Frank Bathgate, one of Andy's older brothers, was playing for the Guelph Biltmore Mad Hatters, a junior team in the Ontario Hockey Association.

Teams were required to get most players from their own geographical area. By moving to Guelph, Andy would not be classified as an import if he cracked the roster. He did not expect to make the club, or the NHL, but he thought the move might help him earn more money for his mom.

When the men who managed Guelph were not impressed with the younger Bathgate and released him, his brother Frank said, "If Andy doesn't stay we're both going."

The Bathgate brothers headed to the train station, planning to go and play for the Windsor Spitfires. But Guelph's managers caught them before they left the platform and promised to give Andy a longer look in camp. He started playing better and stuck — but disaster struck on his first shift in his inaugural game with Guelph.

As he took a heavy check, Bathgate's foot went right through the boards and he suffered considerable damage to his left knee. The damage was so extensive that doctors had to install a steel plate in the knee and, for the rest of his career, Bathgate would wear heavy braces on both knees.

Remarkably, Bathgate recovered in time to score 21 goals and compile 46 points in 1949–1950 as he played alongside his brother. "Frank was really a good playmaker," recalls Andy. "He could really handle the puck. All I had to do was get in the opening and he would feed it to me and I got a lot of easy goals, basically. Being I was only 17 … I just played the one year with Frank and we won the [Ontario Hockey Association] championship that year. We were really underdogs all the way along. I thought we should have won the Memorial Cup. We played Montreal in the Eastern Canada championship and they had a pretty good team, but we got run out of the rink."

Andy Bathgate did get another chance for the Memorial Cup in his third and final season with Guelph, in 1952, when he served as the team's captain.

Today, the Memorial Cup champion is determined in a tournament involving the champions of Canada's three major junior leagues and the club from the event's host city. Back then, the champions of eastern and western Canada squared off in a best-of-seven series. Playing on a line with Dean Prentice and Bill McCreary, Bathgate steered Guelph to the Memorial Cup finals through series victories over a star-studded Toronto Marlboros team, Porcupine Hills, and the arch-rival Montreal Junior Canadiens.

The big right winger, who was as graceful as future star Wayne Gretzky and as physical as Rocket Richard, was simply unstoppable as his Biltmores swept the Regina Pats 4–0 to claim the Canadian title on May 2, 1952. The series became a laughingstock as Guelph outscored Regina by a whopping 30–8 count in the four games. Amazingly, Bathgate participated in two-thirds of the goals — 20 of the 30, to be exact — as he recorded 8 goals and 12 assists.

In the fourth and final game, Guelph romped to a 10–2 victory at Maple Leaf Gardens in Toronto. Bathgate only recorded a goal and an assist but probably would have had more if Guelph hadn't jumped out to a 10–0 lead and taken it easy in the third period.

"The prestige of the Memorial Cup finals must have been set back 10 years by last night's shambles at Maple Leaf Gardens," wrote Georgie MacFarlane in the *Globe and Mail* the next day, adding "Bathgate completed the best series of his career."

New York scouts were impressed with the rugged right winger during that championship season, and the Rangers put him on their negotiation list, signing him to the standard "C" form contract.

"I thought, 'Well, I'm not going to make the NHL, so I don't really need to worry about this contract,' so I accepted it," recalls Bathgate. Around this time, most players would probably look forward to moving up to the NHL — but not Bathgate. He had negotiated a nice contract with his junior team and was earning $190 per week on a $125 weekly salary with his junior team and a part-time job.

Ironically, Bathgate would make more money if he

played junior instead of pro. Unlike today, if Bathgate reached the pros, he could not return to junior, so he was quite happy as he started his fourth season with Guelph.

Then, the Rangers called him up — much to his disappointment, because he lost his part-time job in Guelph and rarely played with the NHL club. At the end of practice on the day before Christmas in 1952, the Rangers sent him to their Western Hockey League farm club in Vancouver.

Christmas Day was the loneliest of his life as he arrived in Vancouver around 10 a.m. Nobody from the Canucks' organization — or anybody else — was there to greet him. He asked a man at the airport if he knew anybody on the Canucks.

"No, I don't, but I know somebody down the street who does."

"What's his name?" asked Bathgate.

"Lou Fontinato."

Bathgate's fortunes were about to change. He and Fontinato had been teammates in Guelph and were old friends and now they would be teammates with the Canucks. Bathgate managed to reach Fontinato by phone and then got on a bus and met him downtown.

"It was a life saver, because I was going home," recalls Bathgate. "I thought, 'What am I doing here? This is ridiculous, running around.' They didn't even know I was coming, so I just went and I started playing a little better."

Bathgate scored 13 goals in 37 games playing on a line

Andy Bathgate

with veteran Larry Popein for the Canucks. Then the rookie right winger was recalled to the Rangers.

New York fans could hurl the meanest insults. If they knew they bothered you, they would get on you all the more. One season, for example, they hanged Allan Stanley in effigy. Stanley would go on to win four Stanley Cups with the Toronto Maple Leafs in the 1960s, and earn selection into the Hockey Hall of Fame in 1981.

To avoid the critics' wrath, Bathgate never looked any of them in the eye when he was on the ice. He nevertheless managed to keep their attention on him as his offensive output steadily improved. In 1958–1959, he recorded 40 goals and 48 assists. He became the second Ranger in NHL history to capture the Hart Trophy as the NHL's most outstanding player — even though the Rangers missed the playoffs.

Back in 1954, goaltender Al Rollins had been the first to accomplish that feat, with the Chicago Blackhawks. As of this writing, since Bathgate earned the honour, only Mario Lemieux of the Pittsburgh Penguins (1988) and Jarome Iginla of the Calgary Flames (2003) have received the Hart after their clubs failed to qualify for the post-season.

"I tried to be as consistent as I could and give the best — and I was lucky I wasn't injured very often," says Bathgate.

Bathgate had a few tricks in his repertoire and thought a lot about equipment. He was among the first NHL players to use a curved stick. He had used one for a while back in junior with Guelph — until he shot the puck over the end screen and hit a woman "right in the mouth," costing the team a hefty dentist bill. Nevertheless, he liked the extra power the curved stick gave him, so he tried it again as a Ranger.

According to Bathgate, Chicago centre Stan Mikita, who also shot right, was running short of sticks one day while the Blackhawks were on an extended road trip. So the trainer gave Mikita a couple of Bathgate's hooked sticks, and Mikita immediately started scoring more goals.

Seeing the benefits, Mikita told teammate Bobby Hull about the curved sticks. The two players then hooked their blades even more. Although for decades it's been widely believed that they were the first players to use the curved stick, Bathgate claims otherwise.

"They really perfected it, believe me, but I did it when I was nine years old," says Bathgate, who first began curving the plastic blade he used while playing street hockey in Winnipeg.

On November 1, 1959, Bathgate helped introduce another piece of equipment, which goaltenders would not dare to go without today. That night, the Rangers were playing the Montreal Canadiens, the most dominant team of the era, and Bathgate was waging his usual war of words with legendary Habs' net minder Jacques Plante.

A few weeks earlier, Bathgate had scored on Plante on a long shot and chided, "Nice catch, Jacques," as he went by the net.

Like all goalies then, Plante played without a mask, but he was becoming increasingly concerned about getting hit in the face with the puck. In those days, according to custom, skaters did not hit goaltenders if they were out of their crease. Nowadays skaters often run them while they are in the net!

If a puck went around the boards behind the net, a goalie would skate out of one side of goal, stop the disk, and skate back in the other side.

As Bathgate was coming around the net, Plante poked

him with his stick and the right winger flew headfirst into the boards. He cut his ear and hurt his shoulder.

Bathgate knew half the Montreal team would come after him if he tried to fight Plante, so he devised a different strategy to get back at him.

A little while later, knowing that Plante would be frozen to the post, he faked a move behind the net — and fired a wrist shot right at Plante's head. The puck hit the goalie in the cheek and cut him for about six stitches.

Since there were no backup goalies then, the game was stalled while Plante went to the dressing room for his facial repairs. When the goaltender came out, he put on a home-made fiberglass mask and used it for the rest of the game — and, eventually, for the rest of his career.

Bathgate's shot and Plante's resulting decision to wear a mask prompted other goalies to begin wearing facial protection. Plante came up with one design that was manufactured en masse and used by kids across Canada. Today, that basic design is still incorporated in the combined fiberglass and cage masks that goalies at all levels use.

"It was deliberate on my part, because I thought he could have ended my career," says Bathgate of his shot to Plante's head. "I always felt that you have to take care of things. If somebody wants to do things that, you feel, could have hurt you or injured you [in] some way, you better not let it go too far. So I gave him what I call a bow tie under his eye. And here he comes out and puts this ugly mask on. To this day, I don't know whether he looked better or worse."

Most seasons, fans couldn't tell whether the Rangers looked better, either. The New York club seemed to be constantly rebuilding, and rarely contended for the Stanley Cup. Most seasons, despite Bathgate's scoring prowess, they didn't even make the playoffs, but Bathgate remained among the league's top scorers every season. In 1961–1962, he and Bobby Hull tied for the regular-season scoring championship with 84 points, but Hull was awarded the Art Ross Trophy as the league's top scorer because he had scored more goals.

Thanks to Bathgate's consistency, in the spring of 1962, the Rangers were battling for a rare post-season berth with the struggling Detroit Red Wings. On March 14, 1962, the Rangers and the Red Wings were neck-and-neck in the playoff race with New York holding a one-point lead in the standings for the fourth and final post-season spot.

Heading into the third period, the teams were tied 2–2 on goals by New York's Bathgate and Earl Ingarfield, and Detroit's Claude LaForge and Gordie Howe. With his goal, Howe became only the second player in NHL history, behind Montreal's Rocket Richard, to score 500 goals.

Eight minutes into the third period, Bathgate's old buddy Dean Prentice, who had also been a teammate in Guelph, took the puck and broke in alone on Detroit goaltender Hank Bassen, who was filling in for injured legend Terry Sawchuk. As Prentice tried to go around him, Bassen suddenly threw his stick at Prentice, knocking the puck away from him and Bathgate retrieved the loose disk.

Referee Ed Powers blew his whistle and immediately pointed to centre ice, giving the signal for a rare penalty shot. Since Bathgate had touched the puck last, the official sent him to centre ice. As 15,362 spectators anxiously looked on, Bathgate calmly skated in on Bassen, drew him out of the net with a fake to his forehand, and backhanded the puck into the net. The goal, Bathgate's second of the game, stood up as the winning tally as the Rangers maintained their 3–2 lead until the final buzzer sounded. Bathgate spoiled Howe's historic night and ultimately vaulted the Rangers into the playoffs as, by season's end, the Red Wings could get no closer than within four points of New York in the standings. However, Bathgate was still left searching for his first Stanley Cup as the Rangers lost in six games to Toronto in the semifinals.

It was only his fourth playoff appearance with the sad sack Rangers, but it would also be his last. The Rangers missed the playoffs again the following season — even though Bathgate finished second in league scoring to Howe. Bathgate, the club's captain, was becoming more and more disenchanted with the Ranger organization. Conditions in New York were less than ideal.

The Madison Square Garden ice was horrible because the popular venue hosted many events other than hockey, such as basketball and boxing, and the rink's temperature was constantly in flux. In all of Bathgate's time as a Ranger, he would never practise on the club's home ice. Instead, the Rangers worked upstairs at Madison Square Garden on a small, narrow fourth-floor rink that had tin boards.

As the Rangers' captain, Bathgate often spoke out against trades that saw younger players dealt for marginal talent. Bathgate's comments frequently angered New York management. Meanwhile, for the past several seasons, Toronto coach and general manager Punch Imlach had been trying to get Bathgate in a Maple Leafs jersey, but his frequent trade talks with the Rangers fizzled.

On February 22, 1964, the Rangers finally sent Bathgate to the Toronto Maple Leafs as part of a blockbuster deal. Bathgate and Don McKenney went from New York to Toronto in exchange for Dick Duff, Bob Nevin, Rod Seiling, Arnie Brown, and Bill Collins.

"It wasn't a real shock when I got traded to Toronto," says Bathgate. "As the captain, I spoke up and they didn't care for that."

Imlach said Bathgate was the final ingredient needed for Toronto's third straight Stanley Cup. Most of Imlach's grandiose predictions rarely came true; Bathgate hoped he was right this time. Because of the big trade, the winger was under intense scrutiny in Toronto. Reporters watched him the way today's scribes monitor Mario Lemieux.

Bathgate picked up where he had left off with the Rangers — scoring and setting up goals. On the weekend of March 15–16, he came back to haunt his former team in back-to-back games. Bathgate was on the ice for 8 of Toronto's 10 goals as the Maple Leafs recorded 7–3 and 3–1 victories over New York.

In the opening round of the playoffs, the Maple Leafs met the star-studded Montreal Canadiens, who had finished first overall in the regular season. The penalty-filled first game was marred with controversy. Timekeeper George Ogg erred and left the Leafs shorthanded for an extra 33 seconds as Boom Boom Geoffrion scored a decisive goal to give Montreal a 2–0 victory. The Leafs rallied in the second game, taking a 2–1 victory to tie the series.

With the score tied 2–2 in the third game, as the clock was ticking down in the final minute, Bathgate broke in on a two-on-one and unleashed a hard slapshot on the Montreal goal, but the puck hit goaltender Charlie Hodge in the chest. Then, with only 25 seconds left, Henri Richard scored to give Montreal a 3–2 victory — and the series lead again.

As the teams headed into game four, Bathgate had yet to score, and his dream of winning the Stanley Cup was becoming gloomier. He finally turned the red light on as Toronto won the brawl-filled contest 5–3 to even the series at two games apiece. In the fifth game, at the Montreal Forum, Bathgate recorded an assist as Don McKenney deflected in his shot, but the goal proved fruitless as the Canadiens triumphed 5–3 and took what appeared to be a decisive 3–2 lead in the series.

The sixth game would be a character test for Bathgate

unlike any he'd ever faced. Montreal never recovered after Bob Baun gave Toronto a 2–0 lead as he fired a shot past Hodge and then crashed into the net and fell down "like a drunk looking for his false teeth," according to *Globe and Mail* columnist Dick Beddoes. Bathgate then scored to put the game out of reach as the Leafs won 3-0. But there was still one game to go — back at the Forum.

Alas, Bathgate did not score or provide an assist in this game on April 9, 1964, but he did not need to. Dave Keon recorded a hat trick and the Leafs won 3–1 and qualified for the Stanley Cup finals. At last, Bathgate was going to get his shot at the Cup he had long coveted.

The finals featured a rematch of the previous season's championship series. The Detroit Red Wings, who prevailed in seven games over Chicago, were looking for revenge after watching the Leafs claim their second straight Stanley Cup in 1962–1963.

In the first game, on April 11, 1964, at Maple Leaf Gardens, Toronto's Bob Pulford won a race against Gordie Howe and scored a dramatic breakaway goal with only two seconds left in regulation time as the Leafs prevailed 3–2. But Bathgate was the goat in the second game on April 14, 1964. Gerry Ehman's shot deflected off Bathgate's skate into the Toronto goal with only 17 seconds left in regulation time to force a 3–3 tie, and then Larry Jeffrey scored in overtime to give Detroit a 4–3 victory.

The series shifted to Detroit for the third game, and the

Wings immediately took charge in their home rink, skating to a quick 3–0 lead. Bathgate started the Leafs on a comeback in the first and George Armstrong scored in the third to tie the score 3–3 — but Detroit's Alex Delvecchio scored with only 17 seconds left in regulation time, giving the Wings a 4–3 victory in the game and a 3–2 edge in the series.

Bathgate made sure there was no frantic finish in the fourth game. At 10:55 of the third period, he ripped a slapshot toward Sawchuk. The puck rose like an airplane taking off and then, according to *Globe* columnist Dick Beddoes, "ducked under the cross-bar as a curve ball drops into the dust." Bathgate's goal stood up as the winning marker as the Leafs doubled Detroit 4–2.

"Hurray," said Jim Coleman, another legendary *Globe* sports columnist, as he sat near Beddoes in the press box. "On that play Bathgate resembled his 1959 press clippings."

Coleman was referring to the year Bathgate won the NHL Most Valuable Player (MVP) Hart Trophy when his old team, the Rangers, missed the playoffs. Bathgate hoped he could give the scribes more to write about — and remember.

In the fifth game, Howe and Eddie Joyal staked Detroit to a 2–0 lead before Bathgate helped set up George Armstrong's goal at 14:37 of the third period, which cut the Wings' lead to 2–1. But Toronto couldn't get any closer, and Detroit was just one game away from capturing the Stanley Cup.

The Leafs faced a distinct disadvantage in the sixth game, because they had to try and even the series in Detroit's home rink, the Olympia. The Red Wings led 1–0 after the first period but the clubs exchanged two goals in the second period and the score was tied 3–3 after 40 minutes.

Then the Leafs suffered a major blow 13 minutes into the third period as defenceman Bob Baun, one of their most dependable rearguards, who was also showing rare offensive bursts in these playoffs, blocked a Gordie Howe howitzer with his foot. Baun crumpled to the ice and was carried on a stretcher into the dressing room. Bathgate's hopes of winning a championship were literally fading by the minute. Baun knew immediately that his leg was broken and word soon spread in the press box that he was out for the rest of the playoffs. In the Leafs' dressing room, Baun huddled with trainer Robert Haggert, team physician Dr. Jim Murray, and Dr. Bill Stromberg, a Leafs fan who was in town from Chicago for the game.

"Freeze it," said Baun, determined to get back on the ice.

Stromberg pulled a hypodermic needle out of his medical bag and injected the leg with enough drug to thwart the intense pain. Only four minutes later, Baun was back on the ice.

The scored remained tied 3–3 at the end of regulation. The overtime session was less than two minutes old when the puck came to Baun on the blueline and he fired the disk at the net. Before it got there, the puck bounced on the ice like a cork and then hit Detroit defenceman Bill Gadsby's stick and bolted past surprised goaltender Sawchuk. Suddenly, the series was tied. Bathgate would get another crack at the Cup after all!

In the first period of the seventh and deciding game on April 25, 1964, at Maple Leaf Gardens, the Wings had the puck in Toronto's zone and attempted to pass it back to defenceman Junior Langlois at the point. But Bathgate anticipated the play, chipped the puck past the defenceman, and raced in alone on goaltender Sawchuk.

Bathgate had a habit of humming instructions to himself. To remind himself about a goalie's weak spots, he would hum "short side high," or "short side low."

"I don't know how many other guys [hummed], but every day [I'd] pick a little song and I'd be hummin' it," he says. "Some of the guys used to laugh but that's what kept me relaxed and concentrating at the same time, I think. It would give me a rhythm, I guess."

As he skated in on Sawchuk, he reminded himself to shoot high over Sawchuk's short side.

"I knew Terry Sawchuk couldn't lift his left shoulder very well," says Bathgate. "He had had an operation … I knew I had to go over Sawchuk's left shoulder."

The shot sailed over Sawchuk — and stood up as the winner as Toronto went on to a 4–0 triumph to claim the coveted Cup. The goal became the highlight of Bathgate's career, marking the only time he was on a team that won the Cup.

He struggled the next season as he suffered a broken thumb, and the Leafs were eliminated early from the playoffs. Toronto traded him to Detroit, where he was asked to play a new position on a line with future Hall of Famers Alex Delvecchio and Gordie Howe.

"They wanted me to be a left winger and, every time I turned around, here was Gordie beside me," Bathgate recalls. "I liked to roam around. I was trying my best, but everything was so awkward. The shooting [from the off wing] and that, I could do it, but playing with Gordie, you had to have a way of judging what he was doing, and I didn't have enough time to really get into it. I never got out of first gear in Detroit."

It looked like Bathgate was at the end of his career, but after being claimed by Pittsburgh in the 1967–1968 expansion draft, he counted 20 goals and added 39 assists. Despite those accomplishments, Pittsburgh attempted to trade Bathgate to Montreal, where the Canadiens' general manager Sam Pollock wanted him to become a player-coach with their farm team in Nova Scotia.

Bathgate was not ready to retire — and refused to report. He looked for another place to play and thought about Vancouver. He had met his wife in the west coast city during his first stint there as a member of the Rangers' organization, and he knew that she longed to move back to her home town.

"I had a tough time convincing [Vancouver coach] Joe Crozier that I was coming out there … " says Bathgate. "I didn't make beans as far as money was concerned, but that wasn't why I was coming out. I just wanted to play and

I wanted to prove something — and go out and let my wife enjoy her parents while they were still with us."

Bathgate enjoyed two stellar seasons in Vancouver as he guided the Canucks to a pair of Pacific Coast Hockey League titles before they joined the NHL. In his second campaign, he accumulated a whopping 108 points in 1969–1970, becoming the first player in a Canucks uniform to hit the century mark. As of this writing, Pavel Bure and Markus Naslund are the only Canucks who have recorded 100 points since then.

The strong showing earned him another season in the NHL, with Pittsburgh. In a rare move, Bathgate then reapplied for his amateur status and joined Ambri Piotta of Switzerland as a player-coach in 1971–1972. In November of 1973, he was hired as coach of the Vancouver Blazers of the World Hockey Association after player-coach Johnny MacKenzie decided he wanted to concentrate on playing and general manager Phil Watson devoted full attention to his management responsibilities.

However, the following season, the Blazers hired Joe Crozier, who had coached Bathgate with the Canucks, as general manager. Crozier appointed himself head coach and Bathgate was demoted to assistant coach. Crozier and Bathgate were among the first coaches to share a bench, along with Fred Shero and Mike Nykoluk of the Philadelphia Flyers. Previously, teams only had head coaches. In the future, all NHL clubs would have a head coach and a number of assistant coaches.

As often happens with players after they retire, Bathgate

dreamed of playing again; however, with Bathgate feeling the effects of a lingering eye injury, Crozier said no. In November of 1974, as the Blazers struggled, and Bathgate's eye improved, Crozier relented and, at the age of 41, Bathgate suited up again on right wing. About a month later, in a game at Cleveland, he sent a shot through Crusaders defenceman Paul Shmyr's legs and past goaltender Bob Whidden for the 350th regular-season goal of his North American pro career — but it also proved to be Bathgate's last. He was limited to 11 games because of injuries, but still produced a respectable seven points, and he left the organization at the end of the season, when the Blazers moved to Calgary and became the Cowboys.

On September 13, 1978, Bathgate was inducted into the Hockey Hall of Fame. In a humble gesture, Bathgate invited Winnipeg sportswriter Vince Leah to be his dinner guest at the Hall of Fame induction ceremony in Toronto. In addition to covering amateur sports, Leah was also active in minor hockey and had coached Bathgate when he was a kid in Winnipeg.

Bathgate also gives credit for his success to another old pal, Dean Prentice. From their junior days, Bathgate and Prentice played on four different teams together — Guelph, New York, Detroit, and Pittsburgh. Most of the time, they played on the same line, so Prentice set up many of Bathgate's goals.

Now in his 70s, Bathgate lives in southern Ontario and

operates a golf driving range with his wife and son. He also remains active in charitable pursuits.

"I don't think everybody should be judged only on their playing ability," says Bathgate. "I think it's what you do for people in general ... The hockey community can help a lot of people out there still."

During his fine career, Bathgate did much to delight fans. Starting in 1955–1956, he finished in the top 10 in NHL scoring for nine straight seasons. In addition to claiming his MVP award, he was also named to the First All Star Team twice and the Second All Star Team twice, while competing against two of the greatest right wingers in NHL history, Gordie Howe and Rocket Richard. He finished with 349 goals and 624 assists in 1,069 regular-season games, while also garnering another 21 goals and 14 assists in the playoffs.

Not bad for a kid who grew up without a dad.

Chapter 4
Maurice Richard: The Rocket's Red Stare

I n the late 1930s, when Maurice Richard was about 15 years old, Paul Stuart, who co-ordinated 40 minor hockey teams in Montreal's Park Lafontaine district, recognized his prowess as a goal scorer.

Stuart could see that Maurice would never be the biggest player on the ice, so he set about improving the youngster's toughness and enrolled him in boxing where young Maurice would advance to the Golden Gloves tournament. The training would prove extremely valuable, because Maurice would face many fights, literally and figuratively, en route to becoming one of the greatest right wingers in National Hockey League history.

Maurice, one of six children in a working-class family in Montreal's tough Bordeaux neighbourhood, already knew the meaning of adversity. His father, Onesime, a carpenter with the Canadian Pacific Railway, struggled to stay employed during the Great Depression of the 1930s and the Richards often relied on social assistance. Although the Richard kids never went without food, they lived in modest conditions. Maurice had to work hard for the basic necessities.

Despite the difficult circumstances, Maurice excelled at sports, first at baseball and then at hockey as Montreal's long winters steered him to the ice more often. To satisfy his strong desire to play hockey, Maurice had to get around regulations that limited how many teams a prospect could play for, so he used the name Maurice Rochon.

In 1936, Maurice was playing for Club de Hockey de Rosemount in a small Montreal amateur league and times were difficult. Jacques Fontaine, the team's owner and manager, wrote to the Canadiens and asked for some financial assistance. When he received a cheque, he promised that, no later than 1942, one of his players would crack the Canadiens' line-up.

Although Fontaine likely didn't know it at the time, Maurice Richard would be that player. But first, he would face some difficult tests.

When Richard was 17, former great Canadiens player, Aurel Joliat, and local coach and friend of Stuart, Arthur

Therrien, spotted him and recommended him to the Verdun Maple Leafs, a top junior team operated by the Habs.

Listed at 5'10", Richard never let his lack of stature prevent him from excelling on the ice as he played right wing, even though he was a left-handed shot, so he could put the puck closer to the net.

Richard spent one season with Verdun and then joined the Canadiens' senior team, but he broke his left ankle and was sidelined for the rest of the campaign. When he returned to action the following season, he broke his left wrist — but he recovered in time to score six goals in just four playoff games.

The ankle injury turned out to be a blessing for the Canadiens because it exempted him from service in World War II. On November 1, 1942, at the age of 21, Richard was able to suit up for the NHL club while many veterans were fighting overseas.

It took him less than a minute in his first regular-season game to make his presence known. Just 36 seconds into a game at the Forum, he assisted on Tony Demers' opening goal. The *Globe and Mail* reported: "Richard was spectacular in his frequent appearances on the ice."

It appeared that many more spectacular moments would soon follow, but only 16 games into his rookie season, in December of 1942, Richard broke his right ankle in a collision with Boston's Johnny Crawford.

Montreal coach Dick Irvin and general manager Tommy Gorman questioned whether Richard was too "brittle," raising his ire, which would become legendary in the years to come.

By the time Richard suited up for his second NHL season after his long layoff, Montreal's fickle fans were looking forward to the day when hockey-playing veterans would return to the Habs line-up from World War II. The Canadiens had not won the Stanley Cup since 1931.

Often, the sophomore season for a hockey player seems unusually cursed; many top rookies have floundered in their second season. But this was not so for Richard, who thrived right from training camp, when his legend started to take shape.

During one training session, Montreal veteran Ray Getliffe was sitting on the bench watching Richard when the young winger took the puck at the blueline, deked two opponents, streaked in on net, and scored. With the war still raging in Europe, and weighing heavily on all Canadians' hearts, the play evoked a strong image in Getliffe's mind.

"Geez," said Getliffe, "he went in like a rocket."

Sportswriter Dink Carroll happened to be standing behind the Canadiens' bench and heard Getliffe's comment. Shortly thereafter, Carroll dubbed him "Rocket Richard" and other scribes soon began using the nickname in their stories. Some historians credit another sportswriter, Baz O'Meara, with devising the moniker. Either way, Richard's nickname would stick forever.

Seeing that a new star had been born, many of Richard's jealous rivals abused him physically and verbally — and observers questioned how Richard would fare against stronger opposition.

Since several players were away fighting overseas, the Habs used a short bench, with their line-up reduced to as few as 14 players some nights. When the stars came home, many suggested, Richard's weaknesses would be exposed.

"He was a wartime hockey player," recalled general manager Frank Selke in one newspaper account. "When the boys come back, they said, they'll look after Maurice. Nobody looked after Maurice. He looked after himself. When the boys come back, they said, they'll catch up with him. The only thing that caught up with Maurice is time."

In the early 1940s, time was a long way from catching up with Richard as he skated alongside Elmer Lach and Toe Blake on the Punch Line, which still ranks as one of the greatest lines in hockey history. On March 23, 1944, in a playoff game against the Maple Leafs at the Forum, Richard scored two goals in the first period and three more in the second period. They were all the goals the Habs got — and needed — as they stomped Toronto 5–1. After the game, the three stars were announced. The first star was Maurice Richard, the second star was Maurice Richard, and the third star was Maurice Richard!

Montreal ousted Toronto and went on to sweep the Chicago Blackhawks in four straight games in the finals to claim the Stanley Cup.

This wasn't the only time Richard scored five goals in

a game. On December 28, 1944, Richard skipped the morning skate, the light practice on the morning of the game to help players get the kinks out, because he was moving his young family from one house to another. Among other items, Richard hoisted a piano into his new home. In the game that evening, he scored five goals — a regular-season record — as Montreal trounced the Detroit Red Wings 9–1. Richard also had three assists in the game, becoming the first player to record eight points in a single contest. That record stood up until 1976, when Toronto's Darryl Sittler counted 10 points in a game against Boston.

Today, great scorers are determined by their ability to score 50 goals in a single season. Maurice Richard set the benchmark.

On March 18, 1945, after taking a pass from Elmer Lach, Richard scored his 50th goal of the season — in the 50th and final game of the season — at 17:45 of the third period against goaltender Harvey Bennett of the Bruins in Boston. Richard then assisted on Toe Blake's go-ahead goal and passed to Lach as he zoomed to the net on a breakaway and scored an insurance marker as the Canadiens won 4–2.

With the goal, Richard became the first player in NHL history to score 50 goals in a season, and he also set the record for the fastest 50 goals in a season. (His record would not be matched until Mike Bossy of the New York Islanders scored 50 in 50 in 1980–1981.)

In addition to his 50 goals and single-game scoring

records, Richard made the 1944–1945 season memorable for yet another reason. He helped the Punch Line finish in the top three places in NHL scoring. Lach was first with 80 points, while Richard placed second with 73, and Blake took third with 67 points.

In 1952–1953, Gordie Howe was threatening to tie the Rocket's record of 50 goals in a season when the Red Wings hosted the Habs at the Olympia in Detroit. Howe had 49 goals and needed just one more to match the accomplishment that Richard probably cherished most. Richard was determined to prevent Howe from matching his greatness.

Coach Dick Irvin's son, the well-known hockey broadcaster Dick Irvin Jr., remembers in his book *My 26 Stanley Cups* how his dad deliberately shared a cab to the game with Richard "to monitor his star's mood." Early in the game, Coach Irvin made the "big mistake" of putting Richard on against Howe. The Montreal legend immediately charged across the ice and cross-checked Howe, earning a two-minute penalty against the Canadiens. With playoff positions already set, Coach Irvin then kept Richard on the bench for most of the game — but Howe still didn't score. The Rocket could thank teammates Bert Olmstead and Johnny McCormack for helping to preserve history.

Howe never did score more than 50 goals in a season, but he still became the NHL's all-time leading scorer, until Gretzky and eventually Mark Messier bettered him many years later.

One memorable night, April 8, 1952, the Habs and Boston were waging the seventh and deciding game of their semifinal series at the Forum when Richard collided with Leo Labine. The Rocket was knocked out cold. He went to the dressing room and did not return for quite some time. With the score deadlocked at 1–1, and only a few minutes remaining in the game, Richard — wearing a bandage on his head, with blood trickling down his face — suddenly walked out of the tunnel from the dressing room and sat down at the end of the Montreal bench.

"You okay?" Coach Irvin asked.

"Yes," said Richard.

The coach didn't believe him, but the Canadiens were facing elimination. Moments later, Richard skated onto the ice and lined up for a face-off in the Montreal zone. Dick Irvin Jr. was keeping stats for his dad in the press box. Former Hab star Toe Blake, then coaching a Valleyfield, Quebec, senior team, was standing behind him as the clubs got ready for the draw.

"Don't worry, Junior," said Blake. "The Rocket will score." After the puck was dropped, Richard took a pass from Butch Bouchard, raced along right wing, swept past Boston defencemen Bob Armstrong and Bill Quackenbush, cut sharply to his left toward the goal crease and jammed the puck past net minder Sugar Jim Henry.

"We all went nuts, of course," recalls the younger Irvin. "I dutifully tried to do my job and write down the numbers of the players who were on the ice when the goal was scored but my hand was shaking so much it was impossible. During my many years in the broadcast booth I saw a lot of big goals and did a lot of note-taking, but was never so excited that I couldn't write. Only the Rocket could make that happen."

The Canadiens won the game 3–1 to advance to the Stanley Cup finals. In the dressing room after the game, Irvin recalls, "Richard broke down and sobbed like a baby, especially when his father arrived to congratulate him. I thought Dick Sr. was a bit callous on the ride home when he complained that Rocket's tears had spoiled the victory celebration."

According to Michael Ulmer, author of *Canadiens Captains: Nine Great Montreal Captains*, Richard went into convulsions and had to be sedated on a training table. He did not wake for another two hours. In later years, Richard would say he didn't recall anything about the goal and would add, "I'm just happy I didn't put the puck into our net."

Unfortunately, broadcaster Irvin notes, there were no TV or film cameras in the Forum that night. Games were not yet televised on a regular basis, so Richard's historic goal was not recorded for the benefit of future generations.

"Thanks to TV replays, future generations will be able to enjoy great goals by the likes of [Wayne] Gretzky, [Mario] Lemieux, and [Steve] Yzerman," said Irvin. "Most of Maurice Richard's greatest moments are locked in the memory banks of those of us who were lucky to see them happen."

In 1954, the Canadiens were playing an exhibition game

against the Valleyfield Braves in the small Quebec town. Richard was nursing a minor injury and Coach Irvin told him to take the third period off, so he took off his gear, put on his street clothes and went and sat in the stands. His presence there was a disappointment, because the fans had come to see him play. Some started to heckle him, suggesting he was too much of a hotshot to play in Valleyfield.

When one heckler decided to get nose to nose with him, Richard took exception and punched him with an overhand right. The fan was knocked out cold and went tumbling down the stairs. From the ice the Canadiens players saw what was happening to their beloved Richard, and pushed headlong into the stands with their sticks and fists raised.

A few days later, Coach Irvin ran into Toe Blake, who was then the coach of the Valleyfield team.

"Is the guy the Rocket hit going to sue us?" asked Irvin.

"Sue?" replied Blake. "He's the happiest guy in Valleyfield. He's walking all over town, pointing to his big black eye and saying, 'Look what the Rocket gave me.'"

The incident was one of many that Richard faced off the ice, at a time when English–French relations were extremely tense in Quebec. He was often subject to verbal and racial abuse and stayed home from bars in Toronto and Detroit because unruly patrons would always want to fight him.

Richard's violent ways on the ice would eventually cost Coach Irvin his job. Irvin knew that the Rocket played his best when he was angry, so the coach often berated him and kept the gate to the bench shut when a referee sent him there to cool off, rather than to the penalty box. Irvin also enlisted Olmstead to deliver embarrassing comments on the bench.

"I always knew how to get to Rock," says Olmstead. "I'd look at Dick Irvin just before we'd go on the ice. If he nodded, I'd get on him. If he didn't, I'd leave him alone. I could get him so mad, but it all depended on the moment, how we were going, who was scoring." When it came to goading Richard, Olmstead treaded carefully — and quietly — on the bench only.

"If I'd done it in front of anyone else, he would have laid me out," says Olmstead.

Richard's temper was as explosive as his bursts down the right wing. In the 1947 playoffs, he was involved in slashing incidents with Toronto's Vic Lynn and Bill Ezinicki. One night in 1951 at a New York hotel, after he had been ejected from a game against the Rangers, the Rocket punched referee Hugh McLean.

Richard's battles with officials reached their peak in 1954–1955. On December 29, 1954, in a game at Maple Leaf Gardens, Richard went after Toronto's Bob Bailey with his stick. In the ensuing melee, the Montreal right winger slapped linesman George Hayes in the face with his glove. NHL president Clarence Campbell handed Richard a $250 fine. That incident was minor compared to one on March 13, 1955, which is still remembered — not so fondly — today.

The Canadiens were hosting the Boston Bruins at the

Maurice "the Rocket" Richard

Forum. In the first period, Bruins defenceman Hal Laycoe charged Richard and the two opponents jousted like fencers. In the third period, the Bruins were leading 4–1 with little time remaining. Although the outcome was no longer in doubt, the Canadiens tried to come back by pulling goaltender Jacques Plante in favour of an extra attacker as they went on the power play following a Boston penalty to Warren Godfrey.

Skating near the Boston goal, Richard took a high-stick

to his head and, with blood streaming down his face, immediately went after Laycoe and clubbed him with his stick. As linesman Cliff Thompson tried to intervene, Richard took out his frustration on him.

NHL president Clarence Campbell ruled that Richard punched Thompson twice in the face — on purpose, although Richard claimed he couldn't see because of blood in his eyes and thought he was punching a Bruin — and suspended the burly right winger for the three games remaining in the regular season and all of the playoffs. The decision, wrote sportswriter Andy O'Brien of the *Montreal Standard,* left Montreal in a "state of stun."

The Rocket's loyal supporters were furious. Richard was enjoying his best season and appeared destined to win the first and only league scoring title of his career. Coach Irvin felt the on-ice officials lied about the course of events during a hearing on the incident with Campbell. However, Campbell's decision was final and Richard was out. The NHL president had a reputation for making tough decisions — and sticking by them when others disagreed.

After suspending Richard, the NHL boss became a victim of his own bad timing. Campbell announced his ruling the day before the Canadiens met the Detroit Red Wings in a first-place showdown at the Forum. Various news reports speculated whether Campbell would be brave enough to attend the game. Would he show up?

As the referee dropped the puck for the opening face-off

on St. Patrick's Day, March 17th, Campbell was nowhere to be seen, even though the president had a reputation for being punctual. Midway through the first period, with the Canadiens trailing 2–0, Campbell suddenly walked in and took a seat while Richard was also sitting in the arena. As Dick Irvin Jr. recalls in his book *Now Back to You, Dick,* Campbell's conspicuous entrance made fans even more restless. They were also becoming reckless.

When the first period buzzer sounded and the Habs were down 4–1, Campbell chose to stay in his seat during the intermission. Fans heckled him from everywhere in the rink as guards stood around him. According to the younger Irvin, who had not yet started his broadcasting career and was taking stats for his dad in the press box, one fan convinced the guards that he just wanted to shake Campbell's hand — and they let him through. But instead of shaking Campbell's hand, the wily fan slapped the president across the face. Spectators cheered and then pure mayhem erupted as tear gas exploded in the rink.

The game was called, Detroit was awarded the victory, and most players stayed in their respective dressing rooms to avoid harm. The chaos didn't end in the Forum. Police cleared the arena and fans – and bar patrons in nearby pubs — spilled onto the streets like a tap that wouldn't turn off. They smashed windows, looted shops, lit fires, and committed other mayhem.

"When Dad left the Forum that night, I thought he would

want to get out of the area as fast as possible," writes Irvin. "Instead, he asked me to drive around to where the trouble was going on. Rather than being upset and gloomy as I expected him to be, he seemed strangely serene and content."

Just as many people can remember where they were when Neil Armstrong walked on the moon, or when Wayne Gretzky was traded to the Los Angeles Kings from the Edmonton Oilers, many Montrealers can remember where they were — and what happened to them — the night of the Richard Riot.

The next day, speaking via radio from the Canadiens' dressing room, Richard appealed to the masses for calm. With his mere words, Richard accomplished what the police had struggled to do with clubs and fists. Such was an example of Richard's influence, which would remain strong for many years to come. Meanwhile, at the request of police and the mayor of Montreal, to avoid further problems, Campbell stayed home from the Canadiens' next game. Many historians and other observers equate the Richard Riot with the birth of Quebec's independence movement, known as the Quiet Revolution. They suggest it was a catalyst that eventually led to the October Crisis in Quebec in 1970, when tanks rolled down the streets of Montreal and Prime Minister Pierre Trudeau invoked the War Measures Act, essentially creating a state of martial law.

After the Habs lost the 1954–1955 final to Detroit while Richard was suspended for punching the linesman,

Canadiens' general manager Frank Selke Sr. fired Irvin (who coached in Chicago for one forgettable season) and Toe Blake took over behind the Montreal bench.

Blake appointed Richard as captain, replacing the retired Butch Bouchard. The new coach, who had been one of Montreal's greatest captains and a linemate with Richard, convinced him to fight less often.

The Canadiens flourished under a calmer Richard and his leadership took them to five straight Stanley Cup titles. These were also to be his final five seasons. No other NHL team has ever won five straight Cups — and probably never will considering the parity and the large number of teams in the league today.

According to veteran *Montreal Gazette* hockey writer Red Fisher, who began covering the Canadiens the year of the riot, Richard was not the best Hab during his final five seasons, as he battled many injuries. Young superstars Jean Beliveau and Bernie "Boom Boom" Geoffrion did most of the scoring.

Still, the Rocket was ultra-competitive, as Fisher discovered first-hand. The Canadiens liked to initiate rookie writers as well as players. Such initiation might be interpreted as hazing, which is considered taboo today, but the rituals were believed to be less violent back then.

Fisher made the mistake of threatening to punch Richard — or anyone else who tried to get him — in the nose. As the Canadiens were taking a road trip by train several days later, coach Blake told team executive Ken Reardon and several players sitting nearby that he never thought Montreal's best player could be intimidated by a sportswriter. Richard glared at Blake and walked away in a huff.

After the Canadiens came back from their trip, left winger Dickie Moore lured Fisher down to the Forum on the premise that a hot story was developing. As he sat patiently beside a table in an area between the coach's room and the main dressing room, Fisher absentmindedly stared at his shoes, wondering about the big story that was set to break.

Suddenly, players surrounded him, pinned him to the table and took off his clothes. Then someone came in wearing a surgeon's cap and mask and holding "a large and menacing" electric razor — and proceeded to shave his body. The "surgeon" never revealed himself, but the glare in his "coalblack" eyes gave him away.

"Gonna punch me in the nose, eh?" he fumed.

It was only a small victory, wrote Fisher, but the incident exemplified Richard's intense pride. Richard "meant everything to his people, on and off the ice," wrote Fisher, who covered the team for half a century. "When he and the Canadiens won, they won. When the Canadiens lost, they lost. When the perception was that he was treated harshly by constituted authority, it was they, his people, who felt the pain and the anger."

His joy was their joy, too — and one of the most joyful periods to date in Richard's inimitable career came in October of 1957. As the season was beginning Richard became the first player in NHL history to be on the verge of scoring 500 goals. On October 17th, the Rocket scored two goals — on plays assisted by his younger brother Henri — to record his 498th and 499th career markers, and grazed the post on another chance as 13,838 fans at the Forum groaned in disappointment.

The fans' unhappiness did not last long, because the Habs dumped Toronto 9–3, and Rocket helped his sibling Henri, the Pocket Rocket, score three goals.

Two nights later, the Canadiens hosted the Chicago Blackhawks. If there was ever a team to make history against, this was it. In past years, Richard had counted many milestone markers against the team from the Windy City — his 100th career goal, his 200th, his 325th (which broke former Hab Nels Stewart's previous NHL all-time career scoring record), and his 400th.

As the game began, Richard looked as cool as a cop in a mob scene. At the age of 36, he was now the NHL's oldest player, but he raced around the ice like a tiger released from a cage. Chicago defenceman Ian Cushman found Richard too difficult to deal with — and was called for holding him. As he went to the penalty box, Montreal's vaunted power play of Richard, centre Jean Béliveau, and Dickie Moore went to work and buzzed around the Chicago end. Moore sent the puck to Béliveau and the big middleman whipped the puck to Richard as he stood in the slot, about 6 metres out from goaltender Glenn Hall. Instead of making one of his patented rushes to the net, Richard fired a slapshot inches off the ice — and it whizzed right past the beleaguered goalie as he instantly became the answer to a trivia question: Who allowed Rocket Richard's 500th goal?

The Forum erupted with cheers as Richard's teammates hugged and pummelled him with affection. Linesman Hayes sped to the net, reached into it and then handed the historic puck to Richard.

"That's one assist I'll never forget," Béliveau told reporters after Montreal posted a 3–1 victory.

Calm as ever, Richard said he was not nervous while chasing goal number 500, but added: "I really did want to get it in front of the Montreal fans and I'm glad things happened the way they did."

For one night at least, the Richard Riot of 1955 was but a distant memory.

According to Michael Ulmer, author of *Canadiens Captains: Nine Great Montreal Captains*, Richard viewed his status as a symbol of Quebec pride with ambivalence. His struggles with Campbell "have long since passed into a metaphor for the battle of French-speaking Quebeckers."

"Before René Lévesque, before Lucien Bouchard, before Robert Charlebois, he was the first symbol in a time for people, then known as French Canadians, now known as Québécois," Rejean Tremblay, the leading sports columnist in Quebec French-language media, told Ulmer. "Maurice Richard was the symbol for the little people, the French

Canadian who went with his lunchbox to the factory of the English Canadian. The grandfather told his story to the father, who told the story to his children. The tradition has not been lost."

"For French people," said Camil Desroches, a long-time Canadiens publicity director, "he was our flag. We didn't have a flag. We had Maurice Richard."

Richard never liked such quotes. Despite his fiery and independent nature, he did not want to be associated with Quebec independence.

"I was," he often said, "just a hockey player."

Of course, he was always more than just a hockey player.

He hated to lose and he refused to quit — even when the time came to retire at the age of 39. During training camp in September of 1960, a few minutes after Richard scored four goals in practice against legendary goaltender Jacques Plante, general manager Selke summoned the Canadiens' captain to his office. "They want me to retire," Richard told Fisher, who was sitting outside the office, as he walked briskly away.

Richard did not go quietly. He was appointed to a front office position with the Canadiens, but management regarded most former players as figureheads. Richard performed public relations duties, speaking at banquets and other functions where he was not comfortable — when he would rather be assessing players' talents.

Five years later, Richard retired from the Habs, and

began a fishing line business and put his name on a restaurant while shunning many offers to enter politics with any party he chose.

Ironically, he actually did referee in bona fide leagues around Montreal, and he became the first coach of the Quebec Nordiques when they entered the World Hockey Association in 1972.

After signing with much fanfare that included a parade, he only lasted two games — a win and a loss — as Quebec's bench boss. Clearly, coaching did not interest Richard, now 51, because he "had no inclination for minutiae of strategy and motivational tactics that are a coach's stock-in-trade," writes Ulmer.

Marius Fortier, Quebec's general manager, felt coaching was a superhuman task beyond Richard's powers. Richard had lost weight and his morale was very low. Fortier believed asking Richard to remain as coach was like asking him to die.

After he joined the Nordiques, the Habs took away Richard's pass to the Forum and excluded him from retirement celebrations for Jean Béliveau, Toe Blake, and Frank Mahovlich.

Although Richard had retired in 1960, according to Hall of Fame goaltender Ken Dryden, he was everywhere — in photos, in the stories players heard in his retired # 9 that hung from the rink's rafters. In addition to his influence, Richard passed on his "get-to-the-net" spirit. There was no question his influence was still felt throughout the Forum.

In the 20 years after Richard retired, the Canadiens won 10 Stanley Cup championships. In 1973, after his younger brother Henri retired, the Canadiens welcomed Richard back into the fold. In 1980, the club hired him for more ambassadorial functions. It was a good public relations move, because fans never stopped loving Richard — including younger generations who never saw him play.

Long after they met him, and long after he passed away, people would remember those eyes and the man. If they were lucky enough to meet him and talk to him, they would never forget him, or the time or the place. Like one Sunday afternoon in Calgary in January of 1989 ...

I was there covering the event for the *Calgary Herald*. Richard was the referee, but as he was introduced and skated onto the ice, players dropped to their knees in worship. It was all supposed to be part of the show, Gary "Suitcase" Smith, the goalie on the Montreal Canadiens Oldtimers team, explained years later. Whenever the oldtimers went into rinks like the Olympic Saddledome and played charity games like this one against a club from the Calgary Fire Department, the praying would begin when Referee Richard came out.

But, said Smith, who never actually played for the Canadiens during his NHL career, the worshipping was legitimate. Although they knew they were part of an act, these NHL oldtimers held a great deal of reverence for the Rocket. When they were kids, they idolized him, just like kids idolized them when they played in the NHL, just like today's kids worship the likes of Mario Lemieux, Jarome Iginla, and Sidney Crosby.

Later, as I sat down to chat with the Rocket in the Oldtimers dressing room, I immediately noticed his eyes. He looked me straight in the eye and never blinked. He eyed me the way a distrustful cat stares, as though he would pounce if I made one false move. I would not be the first to notice the Rocket's eyes — or the last to remember them.

"When he's worked up," Montreal general manager Frank Selke once said, "his eyes gleam like headlights. Not a glow, but a piercing intensity. Goalies have said he's like a motorcar coming on you at night. He is terrifying. He is the greatest hockey player that ever lived. I can contradict myself by saying that 10 or 15 do the mechanics of play better. But it's results that count. Others play well, build up, eventually get a goal. He is like a flash of lightning."

I was also struck by Richard's grace and civility — and the respect former stars like Eddie Shack and Richard's former teammate Bert Olmstead showed for him as they shook his hand and said hello and as he responded with a quiet nod.

Although Richard was well known for his taciturn nature, he was surprisingly folksy as he talked proudly of younger brother Henri's restaurant. I felt like I was sitting on a porch talking to a neighbour whom I had known for years — even though we had just met.

"It's nice to see that everywhere I go people still recognize me 28 years after I was in the NHL," he told me with a sincerity I did not expect. Then 67 years old, he came across as shy and reserved and someone who, that day at least, pre-ferred to be in the background. At the same time, although he had retired from the NHL almost three decades earlier, I also sensed that he was comfortable here in this milieu of old hockey players telling their war stories.

I had wanted to focus my story on Shack because he was organizing the Oldtimers tour. On that day at least, good ol' Eddie gave stock responses, and did not appear to have any time for questions.

The Rocket, on the other hand, despite his reputation for being difficult to deal with, could have talked all day.

After his wife Lucille, with whom he fathered seven children, died of stomach cancer in 1994, Richard was not very talkative. Despite his bad-boy image, Richard was a devoted husband and father. Lucille had managed most of his business affairs and handled the cooking and cleaning during their 51 years of marriage. Richard ate little for several months and neglected his business matters. Longtime agent and friend Jean Roy described this time of Richard's life as "pure hell."

Eventually, Richard found love again with a younger woman, Sonia Raymond, who was a friend of his daughter. With the blessing of his family, she would eventually get much of the proceeds from the sale of his memorabilia.

Richard was able to enjoy life again with Sonia, and they shared many memorable times, including the official closing of the Forum in 1996, when spectators gave him a standing ovation — for 10 or 11 minutes — and he cried for almost as long while apparently motioning for them to stop.

In 1998, after falling ill during a vacation in Florida, Richard was diagnosed with a rare, incurable form of abdominal cancer. For two years, he battled one of the most painful forms of cancer, while also dealing with Parkinson's disease. On May 27, 2000, Quebec and the rest of Canada mourned as he died of the cancer at Hotel Dieu Hospital.

Thousands of fans lined Ste. Catherine Street and applauded as a hearse carried his body to the Canadiens' new rink, then known as Molson Centre and now known as the Bell Centre. His body lay there for public viewing, like a late king or pope whose body lies in state, and thousands came to pay their respects.

Meanwhile, many other Montrealers, most of whom had never seen him play, left flowers outside his modest home.

Governor General of Canada Adrienne Clarkson also mourned Richard's passing as she would a foreign dignitary or member of a royal family.

"It is with sadness that I learned of the death of Maurice Richard, the legend of Canadian hockey," she said in a statement. "It is not only the world of sports which mourns his loss, but the whole country. Canada has lost a man who had an important impact on the history of his sport and who inspired us all."

More than 2,500 people filled Notre Dame Basilica

for a funeral fit for a king, queen, or pontiff, while millions watched on TV across Canada.

"It was an extraordinary gathering," wrote Ken Dryden. "People who in the rest of their lives had little in common sat, stood, walked side by side — people who by politics, ideology, station in life, language, culture, age or team loyalty were strange bedfellows. On state occasions, which this so strongly resembled, many in attendance come representing countries, organizations. All these people came representing only themselves."

In the myriad of eulogies published around the time of his death, many writers harkened back to his intense eyes.

Cardinal Jean-Claude Turcotte, archbishop of Montreal, also spoke of them during his service. "On the ice," said Turcotte, "he was a man, a complete man, and off the ice, he stayed faithful to his values and convictions, and he was real. He didn't have to talk much, his life talked for him. His focus was so intense on the ice. A poet once said the eyes are the mirror of the soul, and in Maurice Richard, we could see the whole man."

As Claude Mouton, the Canadiens' public address announcer, once remarked in an interview with Fisher, fans "will never let go" of Richard.

"They won't, because he was unique," wrote Fisher. "He will always belong to them because he was — and is — so much a part of the golden moments of our lives."

Richard's golden moments were remarkable. In 18 seasons with Montreal, from 1942 to 1960, Richard accumulated eight Stanley Cups — including five straight between 1956 and 1960. He scored 544 regular-season goals and added 82 more in the playoffs, for a combined total of 1,091 points (626 goals and 465 assists) in 1,111 regular-season and playoff games. He was named to the First All Star Team eight times and the Second All Star Team six times, and also won the Hart Trophy as the league's Most Valuable Player in 1947, easily earning selection to the Hockey Hall of Fame.

About two years before he died, on June 25, 1998, the NHL created the Rocket Richard Trophy, which is now awarded annually to the league's top goal scorer.

In the future, the remarkable Maurice Richard will be part of many more golden moments.

Chapter 5
Bernie Geoffrion: Booming to the Top in Montreal

E ven though Bernie "Boom Boom" Geoffrion and Sidney Crosby broke into the National Hockey League 55 years apart from each other, Crosby could still learn a great deal from the former Montreal Canadiens right winger.

When Sid the Kid entered the NHL in the fall of 2005, it seemed like the entire city of Pittsburgh, most other NHL cities, and all Canadian hockey fans were rooting for him.

Although he faced the intense pressure of living up to predictions that he would become the NHL's greatest superstar, he could not have asked for a more supportive reception.

Penguins fans expressed their undying love the first day he stepped on the ice for training camp. He also had the benefit of a mentor in Mario Lemieux. The Penguins' star player and majority owner invited Crosby to billet at his home, and dutifully began tutoring him in all aspects of NHL life.

Crosby's NHL education began with the unstated understanding that, perhaps one day, he would replace Lemieux as Pittsburgh's franchise player and, perhaps one day, surpass Wayne Gretzky as the NHL's all-time leading scorer. Although Crosby posed a threat to Gretzky's records, the Great One welcomed him to the league with open arms, and actually predicted the youngster could surpass his milestones.

It seemed like Gretzky and everyone else looked forward to Crosby rewriting the NHL record books. But he could be thankful that he did not begin his career in a different place or time — Montreal in the early 1950s, to be exact.

Growing up in the 1930s and 1940s, Geoffrion dreamed of playing for the Canadiens. Like many boys growing up in his home town of Montreal, he worshipped Maurice "Rocket" Richard, who was then the greatest scorer in NHL history. Like Richard, Geoffrion was a natural scorer, and he displayed his prowess at an early age. He began gaining notoriety with Mount St.-Louis College as a 14-year-old and continued to excel in juniors with the Montreal Concordia Civics and then the Laval Nationale.

In 1947–1948, when Geoffrion was only 16, he counted 35 points in only 29 regular-season games and helped Laval reach the Memorial Cup playoffs, where he counted three goals and two assists in five games. Although Laval did not win the title, everything seemed to be going right for Geoffrion.

Over the next three seasons, he recorded 260 points with Laval and the Montreal Nationale. In the spring of 1950, after the Montreal Nationale finished its season, he was fast-tracked onto the roster of one of the greatest teams in NHL history, his hometown Montreal Canadiens.

There was no draft in those days and NHL clubs protected juniors based on a territorial system. Essentially, Geoffrion was a Canadien by birthright, because he was born and raised in Montreal and had cheered for the Canadiens throughout his youth.

On his first day, as he was lacing up his skates, Geoffrion looked up, and there was Richard.

"I doubt that I could ever reach your level, but Rocket, I hope one day to become like you," said Geoffrion.

If not before, he knew right there: If he was going to be somebody in hockey, he was going to be just like the Rocket. Just like his hero Richard, Geoffrion wrote a column for a French-language newspaper — and his own play was a frequent topic. Little did he know how many other ways he would be like him — and unlike him.

Fans immediately perceived Geoffrion as a threat to their beloved Richard and all of his laurels. Scoring prowess aside, Geoffrion appeared to be everything Richard was not.

Richard was quiet while Geoffrion was loud. Geoffrion

was credited with being one of the first players to popularize the slapshot (although many observers apparently failed to realize Charlie Conacher of the Toronto Maple Leafs used it frequently in the 1930s and was known as the Big Bomber because of his powerful blasts.) A sportswriter, Charlie Boire of the *Montreal Star*, dubbed Bernie Geoffrion as Boom Boom because of the sound his slapshot made as the puck left his stick and then hit the boards behind the net. Geoffrion also had a loud voice, and often boasted of what he would accomplish — and then followed through.

Richard was always serious and an introvert, disliking public attention, while Geoffrion was flamboyant and outgoing — he loved the limelight. Geoffrion had no complaints with Richard, but he quickly felt the wrath of the Rocket's legion of fans, even though they both grew up in the same city. Simply put, Montrealers wanted Richard's records to live forever.

"He was to become one of the elite players in the league, but it was always a source of concern to him that no matter how well he played, despite winning the Art Ross Trophy twice, he was always in Richard's shadow," wrote veteran beat writer Red Fisher in the *Montreal Gazette*. "The Boomer was among the very best, but the Rocket was everything. Geoffrion lived with it, but didn't like it."

In his first full season with the Canadiens, in 1951–1952, Geoffrion led the Habs with 30 goals and placed sixth overall in NHL scoring with 54 points to garner the Calder Trophy as the NHL's rookie of the year. In the second game of the Stanley Cup finals, he scored three goals as the Canadiens blanked Boston 4–0 in their semifinal series and then went on to reach the Stanley Cup finals — only to lose in four straight games to a powerhouse Detroit team led by Gordie Howe.

Geoffrion went through the proverbial sophomore slump in the 1952–1953 regular season as he produced a modest 39 points. However, he performed much better in the post-season.

On April 5, 1953, he scored the first goal, and the Rocket scored the next two, as Montreal blanked the Blackhawks 3–0 in Chicago to avoid elimination and tie their semifinal series 3–3.

The Habs went on to capture the series, and then faced Boston in the finals, taking the Stanley Cup with relative ease in five games. Although Richard dominated as usual, Geoffrion finished the playoffs with 6 goals and 4 assists for 10 points in 12 games.

In 1953–1954, Geoffrion proved that he was no one-season wonder as he challenged for the league scoring lead most of the campaign, but he was as controversial as he was colourful. Geoffrion was known for tangling with officials, like Frank Udvari, and opponents alike.

On December 20, 1953, Geoffrion and Ron Murphy of the Rangers became engaged in what newspaper reports described as "a stick-swinging brawl" at Madison Square Garden in New York. NHL president Clarence Campbell, who

Bernie Geoffrion

did not attend the game, slapped Geoffrion with an eight-game suspension.

This time, the fickle fans supported Geoffrion. Following his suspension, some even sported signs that read "Down with Campbell."

Richard lambasted the move in his column, claiming

that Campbell had been "unfair" to Geoffrion. Canadiens managing director Frank Selke issued a news release in which he objected to the use of "movies" to determine punishment. During a hearing in Campbell's office, Selke and coach Dick Irvin refused to look at the film because, they claimed, it was provided by a biased Rangers employee. At the time, the NHL did not usually record incidents on film and the league did not have a policy for how such "movies" should be handled. Selke said Geoffrion was "in theory convicted beforehand."

Geoffrion also waded into the public debate in his column in *Parlons Sports*, denouncing the suspension, which the Canadiens chose not to appeal. But Geoffrion vowed: "This does not mean I will not defend myself: On the contrary, I'll always be there to protect my skin."

The same column also shed light on the pressure Geoffrion faced as he commented on his play after returning from his involuntary absence in early January of 1954. Geoffrion had scored two goals — while Richard scored three — as the Habs handed the Maple Leafs their most embarrassing loss of the season, a 7–3 setback in Toronto.

Geoffrion reported the goals "got back my confidence, which I needed badly since the famous affair with Murphy, and I hope I will go on pleasing the fans who expect so much of me."

The Canadiens' management wasn't averse to putting pressure on Geoffrion either as Selke's news release on the suspension noted: "Boom Boom can recoup his losses in the other games and by keeping out of trouble in the future."

Geoffrion did not disappoint his boss as he placed fourth in NHL scoring — two places below Richard — and counted 11 points in exactly as many playoff games, but the Habs suffered a heartbreaking loss to the Detroit Red Wings in a Stanley Cup championship series that went the full seven games. However, Geoffrion's suspension and Selke's comments would foreshadow a much more memorable — and historic — incident in the following 1954–1955 season.

Despite Selke's urgings, trouble would continue to follow Boom Boom — and the Rocket. In the spring of 1955, the fans' antipathy toward Geoffrion reached its peak as president Campbell, already much loathed in Montreal, suspended Richard for the balance of the regular season and the playoffs for his stick-swinging duel with Boston's Hal Laycoe. The suspension came while the Rocket was leading the league in scoring and appeared destined to capture his first NHL scoring title — for which Geoffrion was also in contention.

After the suspension, fans begged Geoffrion to ease up and not score as often, so that Richard could win his long-awaited scoring honour. Never mind that the Canadiens were locked in a battle for first place at the time and needed all the goals they could get. Geoffrion rejected the request — as any other honest player would, including Richard.

"Doug Harvey told me, 'Listen. We came to win first place. You've got to score goals to help us win.' I said, 'You put the puck on my stick and if I have a chance to score, I don't care who I have to surpass. I get paid to play and score goals.'"

Geoffrion garnered a goal and two assists in the next game and won the scoring title by a single point over Richard. But the fans vilified the young right winger for depriving Richard of his coveted Art Ross Trophy.

Alas, Geoffrion's points didn't make a difference in the regular-season standings — the Canadiens finished second to Detroit.

"I can assure you that I had more heartbreak in winning the trophy than Richard had in missing it," said Geoffrion. "The Rocket never held a grudge against me. It wasn't my fault that Rocket got suspended."

With Geoffrion continuing to improve while Richard was beset with injuries and weight problems, and with Jean Béliveau also thriving, the Canadiens would win an unprecedented five Stanley Cups between 1955 and 1960. Despite the club's success and Geoffrion's personal accomplishments, Montreal's fans remained as fickle as ever. In 1960–1961, he challenged their loyalty again as he approached Richard's single-season scoring record of 50 goals on March 16, 1961 — the day before the sixth anniversary of the Richard Riot.

"Frank Mahovlich of Toronto and me, we were competing for the goal scoring lead," recalled Geoffrion. "He was ahead of me, but he went into a slump. We were tied at 48, but Big Frank was tiring and I was hot. He stayed at 48, and I scored number 49 against Chicago. Then, we played the Leafs at the Forum."

Former Hab Bert Olmstead, who had checked Gordie Howe one memorable night many years earlier to prevent him from scoring 50 goals in a season, was playing for Toronto now. In a weird twist of fate, he would be assigned to shadow Geoffrion and deny him the honour held by his old friend Richard.

"And for two periods, Olmstead worked his magic, holding Geoffrion to only one shot in each period," recalled *Montreal Gazette* hockey writer Red Fisher in a retrospective on Boom Boom published in 2005.

But early in the third period, Geoffrion broke loose.

Béliveau fed him the puck from behind the net. For once, Geoffrion was clear of the pesky Olmstead and all alone in front of goaltender Cesare Maniago, who had been called up from the Eastern Professional Hockey League to fill in for the injured Johnny Bower. The rookie net minder moved first, leaving Geoffrion with an open net — but he hit the post!

A few minutes later, Béliveau won a face-off and dished the puck off to Gilles Tremblay who whipped the puck to Geoffrion's stick as he streaked down the wing. Geoffrion would make no mistake this time as he beat Maniago with his trademark slapshot.

His teammates mobbed him and ruffled his hair as he took his place in the record book alongside Richard. The Canadiens fans roared their approval of the player they once loved to hate.

"Let me tell you, that was exciting. The fans gave me a

standing ovation," Geoffrion told reporter Kevin O'Shea for an article that appears on the Legends of Hockey Web site. "I was only the second guy to score 50 goals in a season, and it was great because my idol, the Rocket, was the first guy to score 50."

Geoffrion went on to win his second scoring title that season as he amassed 95 points. The achievement was a testament to his ability to overcome adversity.

Early in 1958, during a practice, Andre Pronovost was checking Geoffrion closely when the right winger staggered momentarily and kept skating — but then suddenly dropped to the ice. Canadiens players were used to Geoffrion's jokes and thought he was playing around. Moments later, he thrashed along the ice like a fish on a boat.

"Get up," Pronovost said with a laugh. "Quit fooling around."

When Geoffrion didn't respond, sports therapist Bill Head scurried to him and noticed he had trouble breathing. The trainer then held Geoffrion upside down so all of his blood would rush to his head.

Geoffrion was carted to a hospital right across the street from the Forum. He was quickly diagnosed with having a ruptured bowel and doctors immediately prepared him for surgery. At the same time, a priest delivered his last rites.

Team doctor Larry Hampson reported that the surgery was a success, but predicted Geoffrion would remain sidelined for the balance of the season.

Boom Boom remained in the hospital for six weeks and then returned to the Montreal line-up in time for the Stanley Cup finals against the Boston Bruins. Geoffrion did more than just show up — he scored both of Montreal's goals in the opening game as they beat the Bruins 2–1. In the sixth game, on April 20, 1958, he scored Montreal's first goal, assisted on the second, and then notched the winner as the Canadiens posted a 5–3 victory and won their third straight Stanley Cup.

The bowel problem would continue to bother Geoffrion for most of his career. He also suffered from stomach ailments that many reports have attributed to bad nerves. On the surface, the good-natured Geoffrion's smile painted a picture of happiness. But many observers believed that inside he was a nervous wreck.

Geoffrion managed to contain his nervousness late in his career but, as had happened with Richard, his goals total declined. At the end of the 1963–1964 season, as Yvon Cournoyer was emerging as the next Canadiens' star, Geoffrion retired. He became the coach of the Quebec Aces, one of Montreal's farm teams.

Although he guided Quebec to a pair of first-place regular-season finishes, Geoffrion lost his job because the Aces were eliminated both years by the Rochester Americans, who were then a farm club for the arch-rival Toronto Maple Leafs.

The Habs offered him the job of coach of their top junior team, the Montreal Canadiens, but Geoffrion declined.

Instead of coaching another team, Geoffrion did the unexpected — and made a comeback as a player with the New York Rangers. However, in training camp, he pulled a groin muscle. Then, during a pre-season game, teammate Phil Goyette's skate inadvertently hit him in the head, and in practice just after the regular season began, he damaged rib cartilage.

Geoffrion was slated to be out for two weeks, but he didn't want to delay his comeback, so he returned from the painful injury early — and scored in his first game in Madison Square Garden as a Ranger as New York tied Toronto 3–3.

"Of all the hockey players I have treated, none has been as willing to play with injuries [as] Geoffrion," Bill Head, Montreal's former trainer and head athletic therapist, told *Globe and Mail* reporter Louis Cauz in November of 1966. "He has an extremely high pain threshold. Too high for his own good, I've always thought, but this is something that comes with the athlete."

On the night of his home debut, the New York fans — who used to boo him — gave him ovations louder than any he had ever heard at the Forum. Returning to the ice after the two-year retirement meant more to Geoffrion than his 50-goal season.

He played 117 games for the Rangers in 1965–1966 and 1967–1968 and then, in another surprising move, he replaced Emile "the Cat" Francis as New York's coach.

Competition was greater now because the NHL had

expanded to 12 teams in the 1967–1968 season. The Rangers started well under Geoffrion and moved into first place in the Eastern Division after doubling Montreal 4–2 in early December. However, when the Rangers then won only 5 of their next 19 games, rumours spread that Geoffrion would soon be fired.

In January of 1969, after the Rangers defeated Oakland, Geoffrion suddenly collapsed and was rushed to hospital. Oakland's team physician later reported that Geoffrion was suffering from an inadequate supply of sugar in his blood. His temporary absence became permanent and he never returned behind the Rangers' bench.

At the start of the 1973–1974 season, Atlantic general manager Cliff Fletcher, a former Montreal executive, hired Geoffrion to coach the expansion Flames. Boom Boom lasted two years before what he described as "too much pressure" forced him to leave his post. But Geoffrion's coaching career did not end in Atlanta, where he would spend many of his retirement years.

In 1979–1980, he was hired to coach the fabled Canadiens. The team was in turmoil following the retirement of general manager Sam Pollock (viewed as nothing less than a genius after many astute deals); the departure to Buffalo of coach Scotty Bowman (upset because he did not get Pollock's job); and new general manager Irving Grundman's decision to draft Anglophone Doug Wickenheiser first overall instead of hometown junior star Denis Savard.

Even though the Canadiens' dynasty was clearly over, Geoffrion managed to keep Montreal in first place. By mid-December, he resigned — again because of stomach-related problems. Geoffrion would never coach in the NHL again. His playing and coaching tenures with the Canadiens would both be marked by sad endings.

But in October of 2005, the Montreal Canadiens helped atone for some of Geoffrion's misfortune as they announced his #5 jersey would be retired — before a game against the Rangers — in March of 2006. The honour came after nine other players, including Guy Lapointe, a great defenceman of the 1970s — had worn Geoffrion's number.

On the other hand, Montreal lifted Richard's #9 to the rafters of the Forum after he retired.

"At the beginning, I was happy for the guys," Geoffrion told The Canadian Press about his number's continued use. "My name wasn't there, but my number was. But I said to [wife] Marlene, 'They would not have done that to the Rocket, they would not have done it to Henri, they wouldn't have done that to other players. Why me?'"

"That was the question that I always had, but now, I know why. They were waiting for a special event, and it's happening. And I'm the happiest guy in the world."

With the retirement of his jersey, Geoffrion achieved a long-awaited dream of having his sweater hoisted alongside #7, which belonged to the late great Howie Morenz — who happened to be Geoffrion's father-in-law. Morenz's jersey was the first one retired by the Canadiens, after he died in 1937.

"When I first dated him he once said, 'See your father's number up there? One of these days, mine is going to be there,'" Marlene Geoffrion was quoted as saying by The Canadian Press. "After the first 10 years or so after he retired, he said, 'I guess it's never going to happen.' So finally, it did, and he's very happy."

At last, Geoffrion's hometown club was recognizing him for his six Stanley Cups, two scoring titles, one Art Ross Trophy as the league's Most Valuable Player, a Calder Trophy for rookie of the year, and his selection to the Hockey Hall of Fame in 1972.

But a tinge of sadness still clouded the announcement on the sweater-raising ceremony, because Geoffrion had a new health concern to contend with — macular degeneration, an incurable affliction of the eyes. In other words, he was losing his sight.

As he tries to live up to a superstar teammate, Sidney Crosby could learn from the struggles of Boom Boom Geoffrion.

Chapter 6
Bill Mosienko:
The Winnipeg
Wonder

E very summer, thousands, if not millions, of junior hockey players from Canada and around the world dream of getting drafted into the National Hockey League.

Those teenagers who are selected in the first round are all but assured of becoming millionaires. Many first-round picks have become superstars and enjoyed long, distinguished careers. According to popular belief, the earlier a player is picked, the better his chances of staying in the ultra-competitive NHL.

When Bill Mosienko was a teenager playing junior hockey in Winnipeg in the 1930s, the entry draft had yet to be established. It was not held until 1963, when Montreal selected Garry

Monahan of the St. Michaels Juveniles with the first ever pick. In Mosienko's era, NHL clubs owned several junior and minor pro teams and secured players' rights by signing them to a standard contract known as a "C" form. Once a player signed a "C" form, he rose up through the ranks to the pros. Although the "C" form limited a player's free agency, it also gave him job security over players who were not so lucky to receive a contract offer.

Mosienko, a speedy right winger, was not so lucky.

Like many young hockey prospects, what Mosienko had was plenty of determination — just because of the neighbourhood he was from. Born on November 2, 1921, he grew up with nine brothers and four sisters in a Ukrainian-Canadian family in Winnipeg's tough working-class north end. The north end was notorious for its poverty, crime, and eastern European immigrants. Like many of the newcomers, Mosienko's parents faced economic hardship and many difficulties as they struggled to learn a new language, a new culture and, ultimately, a new way of life.

Mosienko quickly fell in love with Canada's national game after he started playing at the age of 10 in the Winnipeg Minor Hockey system with Tobans Athletic Club, later moving to the Sherburn Athletic Club.

Prior to the 1939–1940 season, the St. James Canadiens of the Manitoba Junior Hockey League turned down then 17-year-old Mosienko's request for a tryout, saying he was too young and inexperienced. So he caught on with the Winnipeg Monarchs, who played in the same league.

Even though he was one of the smallest players in the league, if not the smallest, Mosienko counted 29 points in only 24 games. Joe Cooper, a Blackhawks defenceman who also grew up in Winnipeg, spotted Mosienko and told Chicago's management about him. Mosienko received a try-out offer from Chicago, and after impressing at training camp he signed as a free agent on October 27, 1940.

Wee Willie, as he would become known, was memorable to fans right away because of his diminutive size. He was listed at 5'8" and 154 pounds, but several writers of the era believed he was shorter — and, as Doug Gilmour would in the future, Mosienko sweated off several pounds of weight during each game, and he used an extremely short stick.

"It was surprisingly short, a stick that looked sawed off, a stick that seemed more suited to a boy of 10 or 11," recalled Martin O'Malley in the April 8, 1974, edition of the *Globe and Mail*.

After he turned pro, Mosienko was sent by the Blackhawks to the Providence Reds of the American Hockey League, and when their season was over, he joined the Kansas City Americans for the American Hockey Association play-offs, producing a respectable five points in only eight games.

In the fall of 1941, at the age of 19, Mosienko returned to Kansas City and was called up to Chicago late in the season, in the spring of 1942. In his first seven games, he scored seven goals.

"He played his first five games with the Hawks, with [a]

lump on his ankle the size of an egg," reported the *Globe and Mail* in its February 25, 1942 edition.

However, Mosienko would have to wait almost another year before he would become a full-time NHLer. Canada was in the throes of World War II and travel for some hockey players was restricted. Mosienko was exempt from the war for medical reasons that likely related to his size; but like many young Canadian men who stayed home instead of going overseas, he was not allowed to travel to the U.S. As a result, he spent most of the 1942–1943 season with the Quebec Aces of the American Hockey League and only played for the Blackhawks when they visited Toronto.

Truth be told, the Blackhawks needed all the help they could get because several NHL veterans were serving overseas. During the 1943–1944 season, Mosienko quickly proved that he belonged as he played alongside Doug Bentley and Clint Smith.

There he produced 32 goals and 38 assists for 70 points — the most ever by a Chicago rookie. Mosienko's rookie points record would remain intact for 37 years, until Denis Savard compiled 75 points in 1980–1981.

Despite his small stature, Mosienko did not miss a single game because of injury in his first full NHL season, playing in all 50 regular-season contests. The line of Mosienko, Smith, and Bentley amassed a record 219 points. With Mosienko's help, Bentley finished second in NHL scoring, behind Boston's Herb Cain, with 77 points, while Smith

Bill Mosienko

finished in a tie for fifth with Montreal's Elmer Lach at 72 points. The little rookie was the NHL's eighth best scorer.

He also helped the fourth-place Blackhawks reach the Stanley Cup finals for the first time since 1931 — only to lose in four straight games to the Montreal Canadiens. The

Blackhawks lost the last two games of the championship series by just one goal, falling 3–2 at Chicago on April 9, 1944, and 4–3 at Montreal on April 13, 1944.

In those early days and throughout his career, Mosienko was constantly a target of large defencemen like Toronto's Babe Pratt, who sought to rough him up and throw him off his game, and wound up taking several penalties. Mosienko, on the other hand, was rarely guilty of infractions.

In 1944–1945, Mosienko did not spend a single minute in the penalty box and earned the Lady Byng Trophy as the NHL's most sportsmanlike player.

A season later, he teamed up with Max and Doug Bentley, two brothers who grew up in a farming family of 13 children in the tiny hamlet of Deslisle, Saskatchewan, to form the famous Pony Line.

They were not put together because of their size. Mosienko weighed about 158 pounds, while Max Bentley weighed 154, and Doug tipped the scales at 145. The Pony Line was a fitting moniker, because several sportswriters regarded Mosienko and the Bentley brothers as the fastest skaters to play in the NHL in more than a decade, which was saying quite a bit considering that Montreal's famed Punch Line of Toe Blake, Elmer Lach, and the legendary Maurice Richard played at the same time.

In December of 1945, Max Bentley, back playing hockey after spending two years fighting overseas in World War II, and Mosienko, ranked first and second in league scoring while Doug Bentley and Clint Smith were in a three-way tie for third with Montreal's Toe Blake. On December 16, Mosienko and the Bentleys combined for eight points as Chicago overcame a 4–2 deficit and beat the Detroit Red Wings 4–2, avenging two previous losses.

Mosienko missed 10 games because of an injury, but he tied for fourth in league scoring — with all-time NHL scoring leader Richard at 48 points. However, Richard played the full 50-game slate, so fans will forever wonder what would have happened if Mosienko had not missed any games.

Wee Willie's adept playmaking helped Max Bentley win the NHL scoring championship, with 61 points, as well as the Hart Trophy as the league's Most Valuable Player. The Hawks placed a respectable third in the standings, but they bowed out in the opening round to Boston before Montreal easily disposed of the Bruins in the Stanley Cup finals.

Mosienko's fine play in 1945–1946 earned him an appearance in the 1947 NHL all-star game. The format for the annual showcase game was different then. Today, all-star teams from the NHL's two conferences square off against each other in February. Back in 1947, the game pitted the defending Stanley Cup champion Toronto Maple Leafs against an NHL all-star squad comprised of players from the NHL's other five clubs.

The game was also much more intense than the modern day no-hitter. In the second period, as Mosienko carried the puck up the wing at top speed, Toronto's Jimmy Thompson slammed him heavily into the boards — and Mosienko suffered a broken leg. As he was being wheeled out of the arena on a stretcher, while still dressed in his hockey gear, a newspaper photographer snapped his photo. Instead of being dour and downcast, Mosienko sat up on the stretcher and smiled as brightly as a boy getting a pair of skates for Christmas! The incident was a testament to Mosienko's positive attitude — and his ability to overcome adversity.

Less than two months later, he returned to action, on December 9, 1947, against the Boston Bruins. Despite being slowed by the injury, Mosienko went penalty free again as he recorded 16 goals and 9 assists for 25 points in 40 games.

As a team, the Blackhawks were dreadful, and finished in last place. It was the first of five straight futile seasons for Chicago — even though Mosienko was often among the league's top scorers. Between 1947–1948 and 1951–1952, the Hawks finished last in all but one season, and in that season they finished second from last!

Early in the 1951–1952 campaign, Mosienko knew something his teammates and most of the other players in the NHL did not know.

His NHL career was coming to an end.

Although he was still in his early 30s and had not yet announced his intentions, Mosienko was planning to retire in a year or two so that he could return to his home town of Winnipeg and spend more time with his young family.

"You know, it doesn't look like I'll ever get to play on a

Stanley Cup winner," he told a teammate. "But I'd sure like to do something in hockey that I'll be remembered for."

The chance to become part of NHL folklore came in his final game of that 1951–1952 season, on March 23, 1952, as the Hawks visited the Rangers at Madison Square Garden in New York City.

Chicago had already missed the playoffs. So had the Rangers. Nothing was at stake — except pride and jobs in the following season.

"We've had another disastrous season," Mosienko told his teammates before the non-contest started. "Let's try hard to win our final game."

By the end of the first two periods, most of the other Chicago players had not shown much effort. Both the game and the season were coming to an end and the Blackhawks had been trailing by wide margins. The outcome did not appear to be in doubt — but Mosienko refused to quit.

Early in the third period, after taking a pass from centre Gus Bodnar, Mosienko raced past his opposing right winger, zipped by defenceman Hy Buller, and at 6:09 planted the puck past rookie New York goaltender Lorne Anderson, a 20-year-old from Renfrew, Ontario. Anderson had recently been called up from the minors because of an injury to regular net minder Chuck Rayner a few days earlier. The newcomer was playing in only his third NHL game.

The goal was Mosienko's 29th of the season. In this post-World War II era, if a player scored 30 goals, it was considered an outstanding season. Although he did not know why, Mosienko decided to keep the puck from his 29th goal as a souvenir, so he crawled into the net, plucked the puck and gave it to Coach Ebbie Goodfellow for safe-keeping. Only 11 seconds later, on another pass from Bodnar and a virtually identical play, Mosienko scored again.

"Heck, I don't want the 29th goal puck," he told himself. "I want the puck from the 30th goal." So he scrambled into the net one more time and again tossed the puck to Coach Goodfellow.

Mosienko, Bodnar, and left winger George Gee stayed on the ice. When Bodnar won the face-off this time, he sent the puck to Gee, who raced down the left wing and fed Mosienko. The right winger sailed around Buller yet again and cut toward the net.

"This kid Anderson is no dummy," thought Mosienko as he sped in on goal. "He's going to figure me for the same shot."

This time, rather than sliding the puck along the ice, he lifted it toward the corner of the net — and it went in again, at 6:30.

"Mosie! Mosie!" shouted teammate Jimmy Peters from the bench. "Grab that puck! It's a record."

Mosienko did not know what he was talking about, but he scooted into the net one more time, palmed the puck and flipped it to Goodfellow. The winger had just scored a hat trick in 21 seconds — all while the teams were playing at even strength.

He later learned that these were the fastest three goals in NHL history, bettering the mark of 1 minute and 52 seconds set by Detroit Red Wings rookie Carl Liscombe in a game against Toronto on March 13, 1938.

After he had inspired Chicago to a miraculous 7–6 comeback victory, a photographer shot a picture of Mosienko holding up the three historic pucks. For more than 53 years (and counting at the time of this writing), no other player would better Mosienko's record. Not even the great Wayne Gretzky or Mario Lemieux or Mark Messier or Steve Yzerman.

"When I think back to those days and how I wanted to leave some sort of a mark in hockey, I never dreamed it would be by scoring the three fastest goals," Mosienko was quoted as saying to Brian McFarlane in the book *The Blackhawks*. "It seems everybody remembers me for that. Hardly a day goes by without somebody wanting me to talk about it. And I'm sorry I helped end the career of the kid goalie, Anderson. He never played another game."

Alas, while he did not anticipate his record, Mosienko correctly predicted that he would never win a Stanley Cup. In fact, he played in just 14 post-season games as the Blackhawks, famous for their futility, qualified for the playoffs in only 4 of Mosienko's 15 seasons with the Chicago organization.

The Blackhawks were so atrocious that at one point sportswriters suggested the NHL should kick them out and play with only five teams. Yet, Mosienko excelled above the mediocrity.

Years later, after he was finished playing in the NHL, Mosienko suited up for a senior team in Winnipeg. He was sitting on the bench when teammate Cecil Hoekstra scored 2 goals in 21 seconds. Coach Alf Pike was ready to change lines when the usually mild mannered Mosienko suddenly became agitated.

"Leave him on!" shouted Mosienko. "He's got a chance to break my record."

Hoekstra stayed on the ice and got another great scoring chance a few seconds later — but he hit the goal post.

"That told you what kind of a guy Bill Mosienko was," Fred Shero, the late legendary coach of the Philadelphia Flyers, who also played for Winnipeg at the time, told Dick Irvin for his book *My 26 Stanley Cups*.

Mosienko constantly downplayed his feat. "I caught lightning in a beer bottle," he said many times.

Scott Young, the late Canadian sportswriter, once remarked in a *Globe and Mail* column that he never met anyone who did not like Mosienko. Young would definitely know, because he knew him when they were both teenagers in the Manitoba capital, and he saw him over the course of his entire NHL career.

Mosienko was a media darling before the phrase was coined, not because he was a prima donna but because, unlike many of today's pro athletes, he always had time to answer reporters' questions. Despite his apparent happy-go-lucky nature, Mosienko was a serious sort, according to Young.

"I had to sacrifice a lot," Mosienko told Young. "I could have gone out and had a good time [partying], but I stuck to hockey because it was the only way I knew where I could make what I wanted to make out of life."

When he retired from the NHL — for the second and last time at the end of the 1954–1955 season — only Rocket Richard, Gordie Howe, and Ted Lindsay had scored more goals than Mosienko. Richard, Howe, and Lindsay had the good fortune of playing on great teams and won 16 Stanley Cups between them.

After leaving the NHL, Mosienko helped the Winnipeg Warriors claim the Western Hockey League championship in 1955–1956. Although his best days were supposed to be behind him, he was named a WHL all-star three times — to go along with two NHL Second All Star Team selections and five all-star game appearances.

During retirement, Mosienko went on to coach with the Winnipeg Warriors and devoted himself to the Winnipeg Minor Hockey Association, the Manitoba Oldtimers, and the Hockey Player Foundation, while owning and operating Billy Mosienko Lanes, a bowling alley in Winnipeg.

Long after he left the pro ranks, he continued to inspire younger people — like Brian Cherwick, who lived in Mosienko's neighbourhood and went on to become a musicologist and sessional lecturer on Ukrainian Culture and Ethnography at the University of Alberta in Edmonton. He also formed a Ukrainian fusion folk band, the Kubasonics, which played gigs at local pubs on weekends.

Cherwick wrote a song about Mosienko's three fastest NHL goals and the Kubasonics recorded it on a CD. The song is played regularly at the Mosienko Lanes, and bowlers often stop rolling balls and cheer as the ballad describes Mosienko's third goal against the hard-luck Anderson.

In 2002, Cherwick sent a copy of the CD to a CBC Hockey Night in Canada producer, while an acquaintance with CBC connections put a copy in the hands of host Ron MacLean. On March 23, 2002, the 50th anniversary of the hat trick record, MacLean played a verse from the song on Hockey Night in Canada while old clips of Mosienko aired on television screens across Canada.

The tribute touched the heart of Mosienko's son Brian.

"He was a very humble man," Brian Mosienko told Mike Sadava of the *Edmonton Journal.* "If you walked into the bowling alley, you wouldn't even know he was a hockey player. There were no hockey sweaters, nothing."

Speaking of sweaters, another Mosienko would adopt Bill's famous #8. While playing for the Kelowna Rockets, Tyler Mosienko wore the number, as a tribute to his late grandfather.

As his health was starting to fail him, the elder Mosienko showed his grandson the nuances of the game on a backyard rink in Winnipeg. The two Mosienkos share a nickname — Mosie — and many similar qualities.

Like Bill, Tyler is small, also listed at 5'8", but believed to be smaller, and extremely fast on skates. And, like his grandfather, Tyler, a centre, possesses considerable determination.

Junior teams didn't want Bill and they didn't want Tyler, either. Western Hockey League teams ignored the younger Mosienko in the annual draft of Bantam-age players, but he attended a Kelowna Rockets tryout camp one year and convinced them to put him on their list of protected players.

"Geez, I was only about 140 pounds," he recalled in an interview with Donna Spencer of The Canadian Press during the 2003 Memorial Cup tournament in Quebec City. "I kind of made them notice me and made them list me."

He stuck with the Rockets, one of Canadian major junior hockey's most dominant teams, as a 16-year-old the next year — and toiled with them for five seasons, until he reached the maximum age for junior players. In the process, Tyler became a top scorer and a Kelowna team leader, helping the Rockets win two Western Hockey League championships and a Memorial Cup national major junior title.

"His heart probably weighed 135 pounds," Marc Habscheid, then the Rockets' coach, told The Canadian Press during the 2003 Memorial Cup.

In the fall of 2005, his junior eligibility complete,

Tyler Mosienko attended the training camp of the Norfolk Admirals of the American Hockey League, the top farm club of the Blackhawks. After playing briefly for the University of Manitoba Bisons in the Canada West Hockey Conference pre-season, he signed his first pro contract with Greenville, South Carolina, of the East Coast Hockey League. In December 2005, the rookie was among the club's leading scorers.

"He's a heart and soul guy," said Habscheid.

Just like Bill Mosienko.

The elder Mosienko retired at the end of the 1954–1955 campaign with 258 regular and 10 playoff goals. At that time, only Rocket Richard, Gordie Howe, and Ted Lindsay had scored more goals.

Although the Stanley Cup forever eluded him, and the Blackhawks were downright terrible at times, Mosienko often challenged for the NHL scoring title and finished among the top 10 scorers five times. In 1957, he was named Manitoba's athlete of the year.

Although he never sipped champagne from Lord Stanley's chalice, Mosienko still managed to gain a berth alongside Howe, Richard, and other famous right wingers in the Hall of Fame when he was selected in 1965. Undoubtedly, Mosienko's record for the three fastest goals swayed members of the selection committee.

"I wanted to get ahead, really wanted to get ahead in hockey," said Mosienko many years later. "That was my one ambition. I wanted to succeed so badly."

He made the comments to a reporter while he was in Princess Elizabeth Hospital, the year before his death. On July 9, 1994, Mosienko died of cancer at the age of 73.

Thanks to his famous record, his determination, his grace, his sportsmanship, and his ability to overcome adversity, Bill Mosienko lives on forever in the hearts and minds of hockey fans — and a grandson who dares to dream like him.

Acknowledgments

Like hockey, publishing is a team game. Therefore, I'm indebted to several people who brought this book to press. Thanks first of all to Nancy Mackenzie, Jim Barber, and Marial Shea for their meticulous editing and insightful comments and suggestions. Thanks also to publisher Stephen Hutchings and associate publisher Kara Turner for again giving me the opportunity to write for Altitude Publishing, and for creating the Amazing Stories series on hockey teams and players. Old-time hockey players are like war veterans. It's important that future generations know about their experiences — and learn from them.

The chapter on Andy Bathgate is largely based on an excellent interview Dan Russell conducted with Andy as part of the popular Journey series on Dan's show *Sports Talk* on CKNW Radio. Most of the Bathgate quotes that appear in the chapter are from the interview. Special thanks to Dan and producer Bob Addison for providing me with a tape of the interview. Thanks also to Gordie Howe and Howie Meeker for being so gracious and willing to answer questions when I have interviewed them.

Most of the stories appearing here were first brought to light years ago by several diligent scribes, including: Red Fisher, Louis Cauz, Martin O'Malley, Jim Vipond, Gord

Walker, Hal Walker, Vern De Geer, Jim Coleman, Scott Young, Michael Ulmer, Kevin O'Shea, Lance Hornby, and Donna Spencer — among others. Charlie Hodge's book on Howie Meeker was also extremely helpful. (Note that author Hodge is not the goalie of the same name who is also mentioned herein.) The Hockey Hall of Fame's Legends of Hockey Web site, which contains biographies and statistics and one-on-one interviews, was also a valuable resource.

Vancouver *Province* columnist Ed Willes' recently published book *The Rebel League*, an excellent account of the WHA's tumultuous seven-year existence, was also beneficial during the editing stages. I'm also grateful to the unknown librarians who managed to put all editions of the *Globe and Mail* — from way back in 1844 — online and accessible to anyone with a library card. The service is truly a treasure.

One style point: Today, Chicago's NHL club is known as the Blackhawks. Through its history, it has alternated between two words — as in Black Hawks — and the current one-word version. Throughout this book, I have elected to go with Blackhawks.

Finally, I would like to thank you for taking the time to read this book. If you wish to make any comments or critiques, I would love to hear from you. Enjoy!

(You can e-mail Monte Stewart at monte@montestewart.ca.)

Bibliography

Hodge, Charlie. *Golly Gee – It's Me!: The Howie Meeker Story.* Toronto: Stoddart, 1996.

Howe, Gordie, Colleen Howe. *After the Applause: Life After Hockey with Esposito, Gadsby, Geoffrion, Hay, Howe, Hull, Mikita, Richard, Shack, Worsley.* Toronto: McClelland and Stewart, 1989.

Howe, Gordie, Colleen Howe, Tom Delisle. *And … Howe!: An Authorized Autobiography.* Traverse City: Power Play, 1995.

Irvin, Dick. *Now Back to You Dick: Two Lifetimes in Hockey.* Toronto: McClelland and Stewart, 1989.

Irvin, Dick. *My 26 Stanley Cups: Memories of a Hockey Life.* Toronto: McClelland and Stewart, 2001.

MacSkimming, Roy. *Gordie: A Hockey Legend: An Unauthorized Biography of Gordie Howe.* Vancouver: Douglas & McIntyre, 1994.

McFarlane, Brian. *It Happened in Hockey.* Toronto: Stoddart, 1991.

McFarlane, Brian. *The Blackhawks.* Toronto: Stoddart, 2000.

Meeker, Howie, Charlie Hodge. *Stop It There, Back it Up!: 50 Years of Hockey with Howie Meeker.* Toronto: Stoddart, 1999.

National Hockey League. *National Hockey League Official Guide and Yearbook 2004.* Toronto; Chicago: Dan Diamond and Associates; Triumph Books, 2003.

Ulmer, Michael. *Canadiens Captains: Nine Great Montreal Canadiens.* Toronto: Macmillan Canada, 1996.

Willes, Ed. *The Rebel League: The Short and Unruly Life of the World Hockey Association.* Toronto: McClelland and Stewart, 2004.

Photo Credits

Cover: London Life-Portnoy/Hockey Hall of Fame. Imperial Oil-Turofsky/Hockey Hall of Fame: pages 57, 84, 120; Frank Prazak/Hockey Hall of Fame: pages 24, 105.

About the Author

Monte Stewart has written about the National Hockey League since the 1980s. His articles on hockey and other topics have appeared in such publications as *The Calgary Herald, A Century of the National Hockey League, Hockey Today, The San Jose Mercury-News, The Toronto Star, Grande Prairie Daily Herald-Tribune, Prince Rupert Daily News, Business Edge, Profit Magazine, The Daily Oil Bulletin, New Technology Magazine, Enviro Line, Alberta Parent Quarterly,* and *Chicken Soup for the Preteen Soul.* He also covers NHL games periodically for The Canadian Press wire service.

This is Stewart's third book. He is also the co-author of *Carry On: Reaching Beyond 100,* the autobiography of late Calgary centenarian Tom Spear, and *Calgary Flames* in Altitude's Amazing Stories series. Stewart has also edited several books and articles and taught journalism, writing, and Internet-related courses at the Southern Alberta Institute of Technology, the University of Calgary, and other post-secondary institutions. After living in Calgary for almost two decades, he returned to his home town of Vancouver in the spring of 2004.

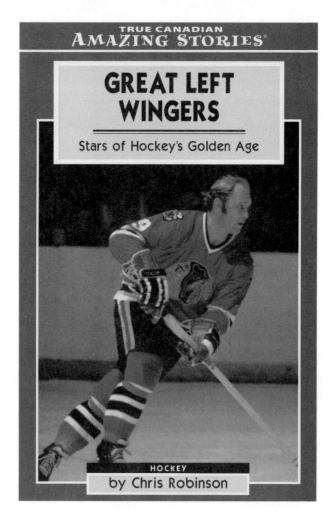

TRUE CANADIAN
AMAZING STORIES

GREAT LEFT
WINGERS

Stars of Hockey's Golden Age

HOCKEY
by Chris Robinson

ISBN 1-55439-082-6

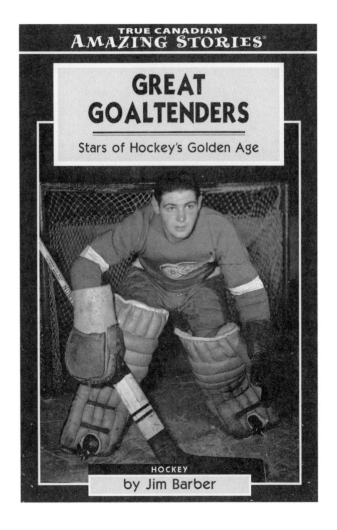

TRUE CANADIAN
AMAZING STORIES®

GREAT GOALTENDERS

Stars of Hockey's Golden Age

HOCKEY

by Jim Barber

ISBN 1-55439-084-2

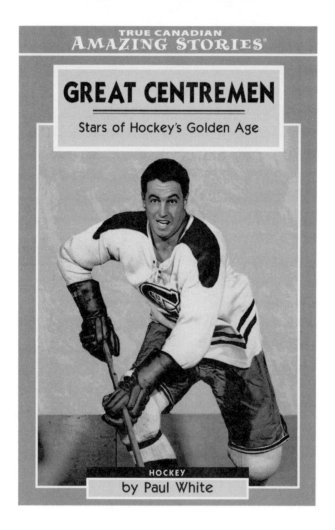
ISBN 1-55439-097-4

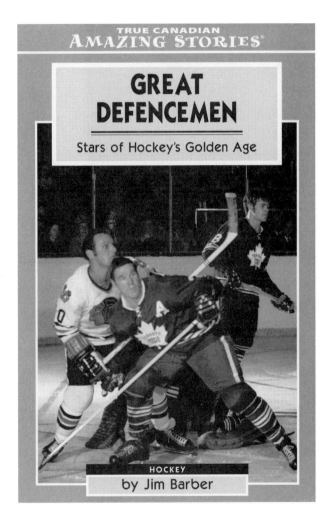

TRUE CANADIAN
AMAZING STORIES®

GREAT DEFENCEMEN

Stars of Hockey's Golden Age

HOCKEY
by Jim Barber

ISBN 1-55439-083-4

TRUE CANADIAN
AMAZING STORIES

LEGENDARY NHL COACHES

Stars of Hockey's Golden Age

HOCKEY

by Glenn Wilkins

ISBN 1-55439-101-6

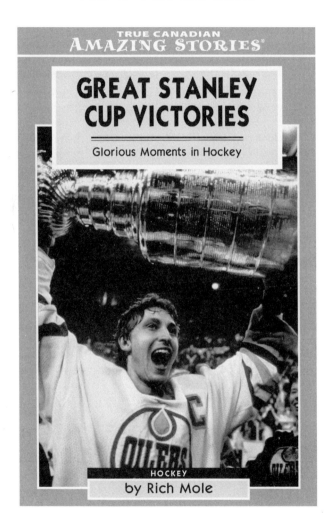

TRUE CANADIAN
AMAZING STORIES®

GREAT STANLEY CUP VICTORIES

Glorious Moments in Hockey

HOCKEY
by Rich Mole

ISBN 1-55153-7974

OTHER AMAZING STORIES

These titles are available wherever you buy books. If you have trouble finding the book you want, call the Altitude order desk at **1-800-957-6888**, e-mail your request to: **orderdesk@altitudepublishing.com** or visit our Web site **at www.amazingstories.ca**

New AMAZING STORIES titles are published every month.